The Witness of Bartholomew I,
Ecumenical Patriarch

The Witness of Bartholomew I, *Ecumenical Patriarch*

Edited with an Introduction by

William G. Rusch

WILLIAM B. EERDMANS PUBLISHING COMPANY

GRAND RAPIDS, MICHIGAN / CAMBRIDGE, U.K.

Published 2013 by

Wm. B. Eerdmans Publishing Co.

2140 Oak Industrial Drive N.E., Grand Rapids, Michigan 49505 /
P.O. Box 163, Cambridge CB3 9PU U.K.

Printed in the United States of America

18 17 16 15 14 13   7 6 5 4 3 2 1

Library of Congress Cataloging-in-Publication Data

The witness of Bartholomew I: Ecumenical Patriarch /
    edited with an introduction by William G. Rusch.
        pages   cm
    Includes bibliographical references.
    ISBN 978-0-8028-6717-9 (paper)
    1. Bartholomew I, Ecumenical Patriarch of Constantinople, 1940-
    2. Orthodox Eastern Church — Biography. 3. Constantinople
    (Ecumenical patriarchate) 4. Orthodox Eastern Church —
    Relations — Catholic Church. 5. Catholic Church — Relations —
    Orthodox Eastern Church. 6. Christian union.   I. Rusch, William G.

    BX395.B37W476   2013
    281.9092 — dc23
    [B]
                                                            2013000973

www.eerdmans.com

Contents

v

Contents

Introduction

William G. Rusch

The word and the concept of *witness* is deeply embedded in Christian faith
and life. Even a superficial reading of the Scriptures discloses that for Israel
and the earliest Christian communities the witness to what God had done
and disclosed in history was critical. In the Christian unfolding of this
story, the community of the Church can be seen as a narrative of the eye-
witnesses and then witnesses to the gospel of the Father's love manifested
by Christ and his resurrection, and shared by the Spirit. Christian witness
to this activity of the Triune God has been seen as a hallmark of what it
means to be a Christian in any age. It is worth noting that this witness has
been described by the Greek word that can be rendered in English *martyr*.
There have been occasions over the centuries when this Christian witness
has indeed been costly.

In the pages that follow, the reader will encounter a collection of essays that portrays the witness, and especially the ecumenical witness, of
one of the outstanding Christian leaders of the late twentieth and early
twenty-first centuries, Bartholomew I, Ecumenical Patriarch. This volume
appears on the occasion of the twentieth anniversary of Bartholomew's enthronement as Ecumenical Patriarch. The goal of this enterprise of some
eight ecumenical theologians is to offer an insightful evaluation of the activities of the Patriarch after twenty years. All the chapters seek to provide
a helpful picture that avoids flattery on the one hand and unfair criticism
on the other.

Bartholomew I (born Demetrios Archontonis) was born on 29 February 1940, on the island of Imvros, Turkey. In the 1960s he attended the Pa-

triarchal School at Halki, the University of Munich, the Ecumenical Institute in Bossey, Switzerland, and the Institute of Oriental Studies of the Gregorian University in Rome. From the last of these institutions he received a doctorate in canon law. Also during this period he was ordained a deacon and took the monastic name of Bartholomew.

In 1969 Bartholomew was ordained to the priesthood; in 1973 he was elected Metropolitan of Philadelphia. Some seventeen years later he was elected Metropolitan of Chalcedon, a most senior rank among the bishops of Constantinople. During the 1970s and 1980s Bartholomew was active in a number of ecumenical roles, including attendance at assemblies of the World Council of Churches and work of the Commission on Faith and Order of the Council. In October of 1991 Bartholomew was elected Ecumenical Patriarch, and on 2 November 1991 he was enthroned as His All Holiness Ecumenical Patriarch of Constantinople.

Often in Western circles Orthodox Christians have been perceived as locked into the past, inflexible in their theological positions, indifferent to the social concerns of the modern world, and rigid in their requirements for Christian unity. In the last twenty years, as these essays demonstrate, Bartholomew has destroyed this caricature. The Bartholomew who emerges in these pages is a spokesperson for Orthodoxy, totally faithful to his tradition, *and also* a deeply faithful Christian aware of the context of the present world and its environment, committed to a broad vision of ecumenism, and a theologian open to the legitimate diversity of the Christian faith in the twenty-first century.

Each of these essays in its own way casts light on Bartholomew's person and contributions to individual areas. From these explorations emerges a portrait of a Christian, a church leader, an ecumenist, and a pastor whose presence in the contemporary world we should be grateful for and take heed of — whether we be Orthodox or not.

Anna Marie Aagaard, a Lutheran theologian and a citizen of Denmark, takes up in the first chapter the topic of the Ecumenical Patriarch in a European context. She points out how Bartholomew views Europe in the present century and sees Istanbul (Constantinople) as a bridge-building city between Europe and Asia. Tracing the history, Professor Aagaard describes how the Patriarch understands the idea of "Europe" and Christianity's relationship to that idea. He believes that Orthodoxy has a responsibility for the creation of a unified Christian Europe. This concern moves the chapter into a discussion of nation-states, multiculturalism, and secularization. In these areas the Patriarch sees a marginalization of Christianity in the European setting. The final portion of the chapter turns its attention to the difficult topic of the Ecumenical Patriarchate in the context of the present Turkish Republic and the ongoing debate about Turkey's place in the European Union. It makes apparent that in that situation the Ecumenical Patriarchate, like other minority groups in Turkey, does not enjoy at present what could be described as full religious freedom. Thus as the twenty-first century unfolds, the continuing quest for "the soul of Europe" persists.

In the second chapter, Peter C. Bouteneff, an Orthodox lay theologian and member of the Orthodox Church in America, examines Bartholomew's role as a leader in the Orthodox Church. A picture emerges of the Ecumenical Patriarch as the *primus inter pares* of Orthodox leaders, profoundly committed to the modern ecumenical movement and its goal of unity among Christians even in the face of negative views of ecumenism within parts of Orthodoxy. Bartholomew's stance on the environment is considered of extreme importance, based on a theological and patristic tradition that has been a part of Orthodoxy for centuries. These commitments of the Patriarch are considered in the light of the present setting of the Patriarchate, for this situation also determines Bartholomew's external witness to the non-Orthodox world and his witness within the Orthodox milieu. Here again attention is given to the relation of the Ecumenical Patriarchate to the Turkish government and its challenges. The section draws to a close with a discussion of Bartholomew's views of his ministry of primacy in the Orthodox Church, the questions of Orthodoxy in the "diaspora," and the ethnic character of the Ecumenical Patriarchate. Its final word is one of appreciation for the leadership of Bartholomew within and beyond the Orthodox world.

The third chapter is a portrait of Bartholomew as an ecumenist, especially in the context of the World Council of Churches. Its author is Günther Gassmann, a German Lutheran theologian and former director of the Faith and Order Commission of the World Council. The chapter opens by relating the Ecumenical Patriarchate to its long history of relations with other Orthodox churches as well as other Christian communions. It then turns to Bartholomew's early work as Metropolitan of Philadelphia in the World Council, including, but not only, in the studies of Faith and Order. Dr. Gassmann then moves on to review how Bartholomew after 1991 as Ecumenical Patriarch has been a supporter of the Council and held before the ecumenical world a balance of commitment to overcoming the theological issues that divide the churches and the concerns for social-political reflection. He notes by examining a number of the Patriarch's statements and speeches how Bartholomew in these texts has revealed a notable respect for genuine diversity within the Christian tradition. The chapter ends with a recognition of how Bartholomew as Patriarch has given a rich meaning to the word "ecumenical" in the title of his office.

Dale Irvin, a Baptist, is an American theologian. In Chapter 4 he provides a history of the Ecumenical Patriarchate and comments on the current situation of the Patriarchate in the Turkish Republic. This material offers a background to review the career and accomplishments of Bartholomew both prior to his election as Patriarch and in the years after his enthronement. From this survey, Dr. Irvin concludes that a helpful image to understand Bartholomew in his efforts is that of a bridge builder. Bartholomew has been committed to forming links between the East and the West, between Orthodox and other Christians, between the past and the present — and not least among the Orthodox themselves. The Patriarch has been active in all these areas, while the chapter acknowledges that he functions on the margins. He and his office today are marginal to the dominant cultural heritage of the West, to globalization, and to much of the world's Christian life. Thus the chapter sees the Patriarch as a bridge builder on the margins. It even speaks of him as an "exile." But it is precisely from such a powerless stance that Bartholomew has so much to say and offer to the contemporary world.

Chapter 5 is devoted to one of the major areas of Bartholomew's ecumenical interests and commitments, namely, Orthodox–Roman Catholic dialogue. Ronald Roberson, CSP, a Roman Catholic theologian and expert on Catholic-Orthodox relations and Orthodox theology, traces the history of this dialogue, its challenges and achievements. He notes particularly the issues around the Balamand Statement and its dealings with uniatism. He also observes that from his enthronement in November of 1991 Bartholomew has strongly endorsed the dialogue and expressed resolution from the Orthodox side to promote reunion of Christians. Fr. Roberson points out the significance of Bartholomew's early experience with Catholicism when as a young deacon the future Patriarch arrived in Rome to study canon law at the Pontifical Oriental Institute. In terms of Orthodox–Roman Catholic relations, the chapter is clear that Bartholomew is both a committed ecumenist and a loyal Orthodox theologian. It sees no conflict in both positions. The chapter documents this view with a careful analysis of a number of the Patriarch's public statements and speeches.

The Orthodox-Reformed dialogue, another major ecumenical enterprise, is the subject of Chapter 6. Joseph Small, a Presbyterian and ecumenical theologian, presents a review of the work of this bilateral dialogue, and especially its statement on the Trinity. While the Ecumenical Patriarch was not directly involved in the work of this dialogue, his ecumenical commitments are certainly in harmony with its efforts and goals. The chapter places the accomplishments of the dialogue in the history of Orthodox-Reformed relations and shows how gradually in the last century these relations evolved from consultation to dialogue. Dr. Small underlines the significance of the dialogue's work on a common statement on the doctrine of the Trinity. He demonstrates the unique characteristics of this text which is able to claim so much commonality between the Orthodox and the Reformed traditions. It is a quality of work that is not repeated in the subsequent texts of the dialogue. The statement on the Trinity is seen as an "icon" to call the churches to greater unity.

In the seventh and final chapter, Mary Tanner, an Anglican ecumenist and former moderator of the World Council of Churches' Commission on Faith and Order, examines the role and contribution of the Ecumenical Patriarch to the ongoing efforts of Faith and Order to assist the churches to move toward visible unity together. From 1977 until 1991 Metropolitan Bartholomew served on the Faith and Order Commission, and in the latter years as one of its vice moderators. He only left the Commission upon his election as Patriarch. Dr. Tanner provides a history of Faith and Order in those years. The chapter gives a picture of Bartholomew's involvement in Faith and Order in this period. This includes his approval of the "Lima Text," *Baptism, Eucharist, and Ministry,* his support of the study on the apostolic faith, and his part in the process leading to the World Conference on Faith and Order in 1993. Bartholomew's interest and commitment to Faith and Order and its goal have not ceased over the years. He has continued as Ecumenical Patriarch to speak out in support and encouragement to Faith and Order. As the chapter concludes, it points out that Bartholomew as Ecumenical Patriarch attended the meeting of the Plenary Commission in Crete and gave the opening address. In that oration the contribution and inspiration of more than thirty years, given to Faith and Order, from a young Metropolitan and now seasoned Patriarch, are irrefutable.

From differing church traditions and spheres of expertise, the contributions to this volume seek to offer an objective portrayal of the witness of Bartholomew, Ecumenical Patriarch. It is the hope of all those involved in this project that a better and wider understanding and appreciation of this remarkable Christian, pastor, theologian, and ecumenist will issue forth.

William G. Rusch

Readers must make that judgment as they encounter the witness of this Ecumenical Patriarch.

The appearance of this volume is only possible because of the support and participation of a number of colleagues and friends in the United States and Europe. This group includes but is not limited to the contributors. Special thanks must be acknowledged to Metropolitan Maximus, now the retired Bishop of Pittsburgh, and William B. Eerdmans Jr., who continues to display a profound commitment to the visible unity of the Church. Finally, my close friend, Dr. Norman A. Hjelm, must be mentioned. He has supported the idea of this volume and given invaluable advice in the long journey from conception to publication.

CHAPTER 1

The Ecumenical Patriarch in a European Context

Anna Marie Aagaard

A brief chapter on the European context in which "His All Holiness, Bartholomew, Archbishop of Constantinople New Rome and Ecumenical Patriarch" lives and works cannot but attempt the nigh impossible. An examination of the historical and current interpretation of the Patriarch's impressive ecclesial title is beyond my competence. Equally challenging, however, is the seemingly much easier part of the assignment: "the European context." The reason emerges as soon as one begins searching for some assumptions with which to reflect on "Europe." What is Europe? What are its characteristics? Where does it begin, and where does it end? Is it a continent, an idea, or, predominantly, an association of modernity's nation-states? Many have tried to delineate its history and describe the salient features of its present, but most agree that a sustainable definition with some objective and common criteria has as yet eluded both the politicians and the academic world. Nevertheless, I speak of Europe; my friends refer to Europe; the news media debate "the new Europe" — and we all presume that we make sense.

Also, Patriarch Bartholomew refers to "Europe." In numerous writings, lectures, and mass media appearances he situates the Ecumenical Patriarchate "at a critical crossroads" with "Bosphorus as the geographical border between two continents, Europe and Asia," and Istanbul, the ancient city of Constantinople, at the juncture between diverse civilizations and monotheistic religions. Except for short periods of vacancy the Patriarchate has been at home in "a bridge-building city" with a foot in both Europe and Asia, and in tune with Constantinople/Istanbul's location "at one of the world's most sensitive meeting points between continents and civilizations." Patriarch Bartholomew is convinced that Orthodox Christianity, and in particular the Patriarchate, "bears a unique role and responsibility within the broader relationship between East and West" and, consequently, must assist in the process of rapprochement between these vastly different worlds.[1]

Europe and Asia, West and East, continents and civilizations; geographical borders, meeting points, and bridge-building. Within these intertwined realities Patriarch Bartholomew situates his Europe and hence the role of the Patriarchate in the currently emerging new Europe. I shall refer to some few approaches to "Europe" within the recent research, but use them as an entry into the Patriarch's own articulation of the complex context in which he, due to history and present circumstances, lives and acts. From Europe as an idea and a specific practice I shall move to a discussion of a Europe of nation-states, and, finally, discuss the European Union, the Turkish Republic, and the Ecumenical Patriarchate. I have no intention of writing a hagiography; neither do I want to promote my own thinking on Europe. My aim is to draw attention to a few aspects of today's Europe and modern Turkey and thus to situate the Ecumenical Patriarch's views on what he names the "privileges and difficulties" of being located in a booming megacity in a predominantly Muslim country.

Europe: An Idea and a Practice

Any attempt to provide "Europe" with definitive borders (geographical, linguistic, racial) is doomed to fail, because Europe, historically, first of all is an idea, an abstract concept, and a notion of coherence across borders. Over and above a formal state membership and institutional rights, citizenship in "Europe" thus implies a sense of a shared narrative. The experience of some community, shaped by centuries of political and spiritual influence from Greek humanism, Roman law, and Christian universalism, has over time been the major influence on making "Europe" a question of

---

1. Bartholomew, Ecumenical Patriarch of Constantinople, *Encountering the Mystery: Understanding Orthodox Christianity Today* (New York: Doubleday, 2008), xxxvii, 134-135. A number of the texts collected in Bartholomew, Ecumenical Patriarch of Constantinople, *In the World, Yet Not of the World: Social and Global Initiatives of Ecumenical Patriarch Bartholomew*, ed. John Chryssavgis (New York: Fordham University Press, 2010), 160-200, focus on the Orthodox Church, the Patriarchate, and Turkey within the European Union.

attitude, and "European identity" thus "an idea unmatched by any well-defined reality."[2]

Some parts of the long history have, of course, shaped "the idea of Europe" more than others, and especially one historical event has made its indelible mark on the Europe that the Ecumenical Patriarch identifies as his immediate context: the 1459 Congress in Mantua. Alarmed by the Ottoman Turks' advances on the Balkan Peninsula, Pope Pius II called for a Crusade against the Turks. The princes, gathered at Mantua, Italy, refused a Crusade, but nevertheless decided "that they with the help of God would expel the Turks from Europe."[3] The word *Europe* here became a marker of Christian identity, and the Mantua Congress buttressed the conviction that the Ottoman Turks had nothing to do in "Europe" as long as Islam was their religion. Historians are aware that the new identification "European-Christian" moved in two directions: "The Christian is a European, but . . . [since the Mantua Congress] it is also possible to use European as synonymous with Christian."[4] Following the fall of Constantinople in 1453 and the loss of "the second Patriarch's throne," Rome and the Latin West gained influence and concomitantly "fortress Europe" emerged as an attitude — Europe for Christians only — which has influenced (and plagued) Western European thinking since the fifteenth century. "Europe" has increasingly been understood in opposition to Islam and the Ottoman Empire, and the sixteenth and seventeenth centuries only added to a self-definition against "the other" — the barbarian, the heathen, and the "superstitious peoples" whom the Europeans "discovered."[5]

Patriarch Bartholomew shares the secular historians' readings of "Europe" as an idea with Christian roots, but his writings reveal a very different understanding of this premise. In a 2005 lecture for the London Hellenic Society[6] the Patriarch turned explicitly to the *idea* of Europe:

2. Cf. Hans Boll-Johansen and Michael Harsmeier, *Europas opdagelse: Historien om en idé* (Copenhagen: Christian Ejlers Forlag, 1988), 7.

3. Boll-Johansen and Harsmeier, *Europas opdagelse*, 67: ". . . in dieta Mantuana . . . decrevimus, ut Turcum de Europa divino adjutoroia fugaremus." On the lasting influence of 1453, see a letter from Pius II (then bishop of Siena) to the humanist Nicolas of Cusa in Berthe Widmer, ed., *Enea Silvio Piccolomini, Papst Pius II: Ausgewählte Texte aus seinen Schriften* (Basel: Schwabe, 1960). Summary in *Europas opdagelse*, 68ff.

4. In his *Historia de Europa*, Pius II mentions events "apud Europeos, aut qui nomine Christiano censentur" (among the Europeans or those who are named Christians); cf. Boll-Johansen and Harsmeier, *Europas opdagelse*, 72.

5. Boll-Johansen and Harsmeier, *Europas opdagelse*, 85.

6. "The Role of Religion in a Changing Europe," *Greek Orthodox Theological Review* 51,

"Europe, it has often been said, is not simply a geographical area but an idea. What, then . . . is the fundamental 'idea' that gives unity to Europe, that constitutes the 'soul' of Europe, and that the European Union is seeking, however imperfectly, to embody?" The Patriarch answers his own questions by pointing to "[the] notion of personal freedom — of the free dignity and integrity of every single human being." This notion lies, he claims, at the heart of what we mean by the European idea, and he adds, "If . . . we are to appreciate the true meaning of this personal freedom, we have to ask further what is meant by a person." Having mentioned Aristotle and the Stoic philosophers of Greek antiquity, he draws on the Christian tradition and insists that "the most important fact of our humanness is our transcendent dimension: we are formed in the image of God." Freedom is thus "not solitary but social. We are only free . . . if we turn toward others, looking into their eyes and allowing them to look into ours."

These reflections on Europe as an idea of personal freedom that participates in God's unfathomable freedom end on a high note of Trinitarian theology: "Our social program is the doctrine of the Trinity. Every form of community — the workplace, the school, the city, the nation, even the European Union — has its vocation to become each in its own way a living icon of the Trinity . . . Such is the role of religion in a changing Europe." The Ecumenical Patriarch continues, however, with a caveat: "To some . . . we fear, what we have been saying about the imitation of God the Trinity may appear remote, unreal, overidealistic. [We do not expect such language to be used in the official documents of the European Union], but such are the decisive inner convictions that inspire our commitment as Christians to a united Europe."

In one section of a series of lengthy interviews conducted by the late French writer and theologian Olivier Clément,[7] Patriarch Bartholomew comments on "Europe," its origin and more recent history. These reflections, published in the late 1990s, focus on the idea of "the other," but "the other" not as "the adversary" of the Mantua Congress: "The origin and meaning of Europe is the person. And let us not forget: a person requires communion." The theological concept of the human being as a person in

---

nos. 1-4 (2006): 338-350. In this paragraph and the next I quote from pages 344-347. An edited version of the address is in *In the World, Yet Not of the World,* 109-120.

7. Olivier Clément, *Conversations with Ecumenical Patriarch Bartholomew I,* trans. Paul Meyendorff (Crestwood, NY: St. Vladimir's Seminary Press, 1997). In the next several paragraphs I quote from pages 153-170.

communion sets "Europe" off from traditional societies in which "the 'other' as other does not exist," and, so the Patriarch claims, the Christian gospel — "the mystery of the 'Other' inscribed in the heart of Unity" — consequently belongs to the very earliest beginnings of European identity. The medieval adumbrations of guaranteed rights, freedom, and democratic structures, and the Enlightenment's push toward elected governments and civil rights subsequently made the European culture appear as "the first open culture in history" with "no other implicit philosophy than a philosophy of the 'other' welcomed in his otherness." The reverse was, however, also the case. The gospel not only influenced history. It became abused by history: "[T]he intimate connection between Christianity and power tended to turn 'religion' into an ideology imposed within a closed society. Christian societies have sinned against the freedom of the spirit. They have denounced, persecuted, or attacked the 'other,' the heretic, the Jew, the Muslim."

Turning to modern Europe and the processes of secularization, the conversations "On Europe" characterize "modern Europe . . . [as] born from a double opposition: that of the 'rights' of God versus man, and that of the 'rights' of man versus God . . . In this fashion a new culture was formed, heterogeneous, multiple, never complete, self-critical by nature, never self-assured, hardworking, energized by research, by polemics, by diversity — all of which create tensions . . . and impetus for change." Religious freedom and pluralism have, as the Patriarch puts it in another context, an immense moral and social value as confirming the incomprehensible breadth, grandeur, and mystery of God's freedom as well as God's respect for human freedom. Human rights, he insists, are not merely the offering of European Enlightenment. They are an integral part of the Christian faith, because faith and tolerance share the same language, whose alphabet is freedom.[8]

Clément's interviews with the Patriarch include a quote from the message of the 1992 Synaxis of Orthodox primates. It highlights the rapid progress of technology and science in the twentieth century and the concomitant destruction of nature, the misery of hungry people, and the danger of transforming "the human being into a thing, a controlled object, manipulated by those with power." But the conversation continues: "It is ridiculous to think that Orthodoxy opposes the West . . . Orthodoxy believes . . . that the West places an excessive value on material progress, a

---

8. Bartholomew, *Encountering the Mystery*, 140.

progress that also harms the spiritual life of humanity . . . [But] Orthodoxy shares the responsibility of creating a unified Europe. It is an integral part of a Christian Europe." In other words, "The task is to turn Europe into a peculiar laboratory, beyond a secularized modernity." Although the Patriarchate has little direct influence on the actual politics of the European Union, His All Holiness makes his pastoral office serve a spiritual vision, not engulfed in secular power struggles, for the totality of Europe. Far from issuing a flat "no" to "Europe as an idea" rooted in respect for "the other," freedom of the spirit, and a pluralistic democracy, Christians must seek to reorient Christian Europe from within.

According to the Patriarch it will demand applying the power of the Holy Spirit — a practice characterized by "that which is free and cannot be assimilated." Christians, he insists, must not expect the church to provide the answers to everything, but "it must make society think," and this will imply recognizing three fundamental attitudes as part and parcel of the idea of Europe: repentance (necessary after the many wars and persecutions among the nations), self-limitation (in order to share with the poorer nations of the planet), and respect for the earth. In other words, a practice of nonviolence, philanthropy, and environmentalism.[9] By his own admission the Ecumenical Patriarch predominantly addresses some of the more radical challenges of our time, including poverty, racism, fundamentalism, and conflict, but he is aware that the list of sociopolitical problems which need to be resolved is much, much longer. More than half of his 2008 book *Encountering the Mystery: Understanding Orthodox Christianity Today*[10] expands on the Ecumenical Patriarchate's concrete efforts to transform the world and articulate an up-to-date Orthodox social ethics concerned with the natural environment and human welfare, the complexities of global economics, justice as the prerequisite for a new world order, and the ramifications of moral corruption. The thinking is permeated by a fervent faith commitment expressed in simple terms:

> The way we work, the salaries we earn, the houses we construct, the cars we drive, the money we spend, the luxuries we enjoy, the goods we consume, the resources we waste, even the channels we decide to watch or ignore on the television — all of these, we now know, impact directly our neighbors within our own society, in our neighborhood, and more

9. Cf. "A Changeless Faith for a Changing World," *Origins* 39, no. 24 (November 2009): 396.

10. Bartholomew, *Encountering the Mystery*, esp. 149.

broadly in our world. Our way of living, we now know, either enhances or endangers the rest of the earth's inhabitants as well as future generations. Perhaps this is the unique responsibility and historical privilege that we share as human beings in the twenty-first century. Are we prepared to assume this responsibility and accept this challenge?[11]

A Europe of Nation-States

When telling the story of the origins of the modern European state, German historian Wolfgang Reinhard argues that "the State" may well be the most effective concentration of power as yet invented by human beings.[12] He identifies the endless wars and the concomitant organization of taxation as the mechanisms that began transforming a medieval Europe of kings and small city republics into what in the nineteenth and twentieth centuries would become a modern Europe of nation-states. It began with wars and taxation, but effective taxation demanded some sort of consensus from taxpayers (assemblies of the estates, the adumbrations of the modern parliament, came into existence), and as the tax collection was often too slow for financing the armies, the cities with their emerging banking systems became involved in building a state with monopoly on declaring war and collecting taxes.

The city culture of early modernity also created a new class of lawyers responsible for using the rediscovered Roman law to bolster the efforts of the state-building powers. Roman law provided, however, every free man with absolute possession of his own person, its rights and property, and as passed on by the medieval Roman Catholic Church and later developed by the humanists of the Renaissance, the traditions and institutions of Roman law came to influence also modernity's secular states. "The unique political culture of the emerging modern State depended to a large extent on the political traditions of Antiquity: Politics in the modern sense as action in the interest of the public arose among the ancient Greeks as a system created by the public." But with the Ottoman conquest of Constantinople (1453), it was not least Roman law and Christian claims of ecclesial autonomy that gave European modernity's emerging state its unique political

11. Bartholomew, *Encountering the Mystery,* 156. For an overview of the Patriarch's efforts, see the Introduction to Bartholomew, *In the World, Yet Not of the World.*

12. Wolfgang Reinhard, "Das Vorbild aus Europa," *Welt-Sichten* 12 (2010): 28-32.

culture: a "duality of religion and politics, in modern parlance: of church and state." Church autonomy was, however, gradually curtailed. In post-Reformation times the churches, often transformed into state churches, were made dependent on the state as the sole source of making and upholding the law, and eventually also the human rights of the French Revolution became incorporated in the European constitutions and thus subjected to the state's monopoly as lawmaker.

Effective Muslim separation of Byzantine culture from the continuations of the Roman Empire, the establishment of a "third Rome" in Moscow, and the Reformation's divide of Western Christianity impacted modernity's emerging European state, but most significant were the ways of thinking and interrelating promoted by the Enlightenment and the convulsions of the French Revolution: "For the very first time in history, a purely secular state arose, which abandoned and set aside the divine guarantee and divine ordering of the political sector . . . religion and faith belonged to the realm of feelings and not to that of reason. God and his will ceased to be relevant in public life."[13]

According to Reinhard, the current modern state can be defined by six characteristics. First, it has immediate authority over all its citizens. Second, as a state identifying with a specific nation, it is an end to itself; but, third, it is normally bound by its constitution. Fourth, it upholds (at least in principle) political democracy and international human rights conventions. Fifth, it is a secular state with no religious justification for the welfare it provides. Finally, it is a huge, historically unique, accumulation of power.

And yet it is crumbling. The homogeneous nations of the eighteenth and nineteenth centuries supported the state and provided it with a social cohesion (religious, ethnic, and cultural), but such collective identity is rapidly disappearing. Reinhard identifies two major reasons: first, the overstretching of the state (e.g., the welfare state has reached the limits of financial viability); and, second, the erosion of the complex political culture that was instrumental in developing and upholding the modern State (e.g., the Greek-Roman-Christian idea that the common good takes precedence). The state's monopoly on power and its possibility of pursuing a specific national interest are at present being curtailed partly by the communicative power yielded by a host of national and international actors

---

13. Joseph Ratzinger, *Europe: Today and Tomorrow* (San Francisco: Ignatius Press, 2007), 21.

defending "the public interest" and partly by reemerging propensities for giving collective and individual identity a religious foundation.[14]

Patriarch Bartholomew is acutely aware of the ongoing erosion of the power of sovereign national governments. In the midst of a "painful process of unification" there is, in Europe, much resignation, troubles relating to nationalism and soaring crime rates, and apparently no visions of the future apart from protecting Europe's riches from the "menace" and "invasion" of peoples from the South.[15] He attributes, in the first place, the decline of centralized state power to the global economic activities that diminish the influence of the nation-states while augmenting the power of economically strong international corporations.[16] Two other influences are, however, equally decisive.

On Nation-States and Multiculturalism

Repeatedly Patriarch Bartholomew points to multiculturalism and secularization as predominant features of the current changes:

> First, the national boundaries separating one European country from another are becoming less sharp and clearly defined, and this is happening on many different levels, political, economic, and social. None of us are living anymore in a monolithic, pan-ethnic cultural milieu; all of us belong to or find ourselves cast into broader cultural currents . . . One aspect of this multicultural trend is the ever-increasing scale of immigration. In Europe today, for example, there are between fifteen and twenty million Muslims . . . Along with multiculturalism, a second major feature in today's changing Europe is the growth of secularism.[17]

Far from merely lamenting multiculturalism, His All Holiness sees it "not as a threat but as an opportunity" which may make Europeans recognize that "we belong to one another and need each other. Nations in the contemporary world are not self-sufficient but interdependent." National

---

14. Cf. Konrad Raiser, *Religion Macht Politik: Auf der Suche nach einer zukunftsfähigen Weltordnung* (Frankfurt am Main: Otto Lembeck, 2010), esp. 249ff.

15. Clément, *Conversations with Ecumenical Patriarch Bartholomew I*, 168; Bartholomew, *In the World, Yet Not of the World*, 121.

16. Bartholomew, *Encountering the Mystery*, 158-163.

17. Bartholomew, "The Role of Religion in a Changing Europe," 338-341.

identity and loyalty to homeland should not disappear, but rather the closed nationalism of the nineteenth-century German Romanticism, which not least in the Balkans made the people of God a dimension of the nation, turned traditional forms of ecclesial self-governing churches (autocephaly) into separatist "autocephalism," and confused ethnic and religious identity.[18] The Ecumenical Patriarch does not hide that, in his estimation, this was an extreme "blood and soil" nationalism, dressed up as pseudo-religion, which showed its ugly xenophobic head during the recent Balkan wars and divided Orthodox Christians. He is concerned that European Orthodoxy too often appears to be "a conglomerate of churches which, though sharing the same faith, live in isolation, or even confront each other under the impulse of excessive nationalism," and he is emphatic in his assertion that "[r]eligious nationalism is the Orthodox form of secularization."[19] Against such nationalism the Patriarch is insistent on upholding national identities in a multicultural context and having the Ecumenical Patriarchate act as a bulwark of faith against all crimes in the name of religion — crimes which themselves are crimes against religion (cf. the Bosphorus Declaration).[20]

In the context of decrying pseudo-religious nationalism the Patriarch has often referred to the European Union as an antidote:

> The most striking contemporary expression of . . . multiculturalism is . . . the emergence of the European Union . . . As a Turkish citizen, we would like . . . to express our hope that in due course Turkey will become a full member of the EU, when the necessary preconditions of such membership have been met, including in particular the recognition of religious and other rights of minority communities. The admission of Turkey to the EU, so we are convinced, will significantly contribute to rapprochement and reconciliation between the Muslim world and the West.[21]

In the eyes of the Patriarch European integration is a "great historic mission to organize the peoples of Europe in peace, justice, and democracy

---

18. Cf. *Konflikt und Kooperation, Herder Korrespondenz Spezial 2* (2010): 47-51, and his speech at Tufts University, October 1997: "We accept the reality of the nation-state, but we categorically reject systems of repression and oppression that are premised on parochial nationalism . . . ," *In the World, Yet Not of the World*, 26.

19. Clément, *Conversations with Ecumenical Patriarch Bartholomew I*, 151, 160.

20. The full text is in Bartholomew, *In the World, Yet Not of the World*, 299-302.

21. "The Role of Religion in a Changing Europe," 338-341.

[with] a shared aspect in its struggle for . . . a common understanding of life, of the sanctity of the human person, and in the reconciliation . . . of diverse peoples, religions, and cultures."[22] The Patriarch's assessment of the European Union as a union of minorities learning to live with common values does not overlook that nothing totally innocent or incidental happens in the corridors of power, but the Orthodox Church can, he claims, become

> [a] force of unity, a stabilizing factor and an essential component in the ongoing process to create a new European reality bridging the Eastern and Western Christian cultures and traditions of the continent . . . [The Ecumenical Patriarchate's unwavering support of Turkey's membership in the European Union] is linked to the belief that Europe will benefit greatly by integrating a predominantly Muslim country, willing of course to adopt European principles such as respect for religious freedoms and minority rights.[23]

It is not easy to determine what is the "chicken" and what is the "egg" in the Patriarch's combination of multiculturalism, the European Union, and Turkish membership, but it is clear that he attributes a uniting Europe — committed to democracy, human rights, and religious freedom — both to the idea of a Christian Europe and to the processes of secularization that over time have emancipated political, social, and cultural spheres from ideological dominance and religious fanaticism. "Secularization is, simultaneously, a daughter of Athens and Jerusalem," the Patriarch claims. It helped develop the modern state with the political and social structures which respect the religious convictions of its citizens. It permitted scientific research, avoided drowning God in sacred nature, achieved personal freedoms and the emancipation of women, and thus "it is not alien to us Christians."[24]

On Church, State, and Secularism

When Patriarch Bartholomew examines the growth of secularism as a second major feature of today's changing Europe, he will sometimes refer to

---

22. *In the World, Yet Not of the World*, 195.
23. "The Role of Religion in a Changing Europe," 343.
24. Clément, *Conversations with Ecumenical Patriarch Bartholomew I*, 158.

the marginalization of Christianity in the life and educational systems of European societies, and he does not hide his disappointment that the latest version of the European Constitutional Treaty, despite protests from churches, does not refer explicitly to Christianity's impact on the formation of modern Europe. It would, however, be wrong, he argues, to concentrate on only the negative aspects of secularization and forget the freedoms it brought — not least the freedom of religious association and that of conscience: "A modern and democratic political and social structure has to respect the religious wishes and sentiments of its citizens. Religious freedoms cannot be curtailed in the name of secularism."[25] It is easy to detect his preference for multiculturalism and minority rights in a predominantly Muslim country when he defends "an authentic secularism" that "is not hostile to the churches, but . . . is open, capable of accepting them as recognized and, of course, respected partners." "In a truly secular culture," he claims,

> one will hear about the Bible in schools, about the Fathers of the Church in classes on the history of thought, and young people will be familiarized with the immense cultural and cultic heritage of Christianity . . . And what we say concerning the Bible — which should apply, of course, to Christian minorities in Muslim countries — applies also to the Koran with respect to Muslim minorities in predominantly Christian countries . . . Let the churches be guarantors of the faith of others, the guarantors of also those who have no faith . . . Let [the churches] be the guardian of the open man [sic] in an open culture.[26]

Such acceptance of multiculturalism and secularization as basic features of today's Europe will demand a revisiting of the traditional systems of regulating the relation between the state and organized religion. Two of these systems are currently operative in the European Union, the Patriarch notes.[27] He names them "the confessional system, whereby the state gives official recognition to one particular religion or Church," and "the nonconfessional system, whereby the state is separated from religion, and assumes an attitude of neutrality towards all expressions of religious beliefs and practice." The inherited confessional system, with its commitment to

25. "The Role of Religion in a Changing Europe," 341.

26. Clément, *Conversations with Ecumenical Patriarch Bartholomew I,* 166-167.

27. "The Role of Religion in a Changing Europe." In this paragraph I quote from 347-350.

one organized religion, is currently being loosened up in Great Britain, Denmark, and Greece, but these countries still assign a "special position to one religious body," and although the nonconfessional system prevails in most European countries, there is also within this system a general acceptance of the public role of the churches and other forms of organized religion. Even in nonconfessional countries there is usually "no attempt to establish a total separation between religion and the state." Instead of "separation," Patriarch Bartholomew would rather speak of "mutual respect and cooperation," and he identifies the phrase with the most important key term of Orthodox political philosophy: *symphonia,* that is, concord or harmony. One may question whether the substance of Emperor Justinian's Sixth Novel can bridge the gap between the sixth and the twenty-first centuries, but if the key words of the novel — a happy concord — are interpreted as "active collaboration," it does indicate the Patriarch's preference for a relationship between state and religion that is "far more dynamic and creative" than "separation, neutrality, or mutual tolerance."

Three European Systems

Recent research in "law and religion"[28] identifies three patterns of relationship between state and religion in "the new Europe." These patterns do not exist in a pure form, but they share a complex context of secular "demoralization" of the public discourse and a "remoralization" of individual aspirations to collective identity. Organized religion has lost the capacity to control individual lives and the discourses of the public square, but, simultaneously, it "offers a frame that shapes and supports different collective interests, desires and aspirations . . . [Religions] are becoming today what Nations were in the nineteenth century: a catalyst for different needs and hopes." But religion is not boxed in by borders. Europe's reemerging religion is characterized by being a "fusion religion," composed by the individuals from different belief systems and cultural histories.

Silvio Ferrari describes three patterns of state-religion relations in Europe by referring to their dominant characteristics. First, England offers a

28. Cf. Lisbet Chrisoffersen, Kjell Å. Modéer, and Svend Andersen, eds., *Law and Religion in the Twenty-First Century: Nordic Perspectives* (Copenhagen: DJ/SOF Publishing, 2010), esp. Silvio Ferrari, "Introduction to the European Church and State Discourses," 23-41. In the following paragraphs I have quoted from pages 25, 26, 31, and 29, in that order. I owe the phrase "fusion religion" to editor-in-chief Erik Bjerager, *Kr. Dagblad,* Copenhagen.

prime example of "unity in diversity," based on the postmodern conviction that homogeneity is a thing of the past. "In a multicultural and multi-religious society, social cohesion can be founded only on different and even competing sets of values." "[The] national State recognizes its inability to forget the identity of its citizens and gives up this claim, limiting itself to providing the legal framework necessary for peaceful coexistence of different individuals and groups." A common interest in a plural legal framework provides the needed social cohesion — as long as there is a common interest able to resist "the centrifugal forces generated by the growing plurality." At the time of writing this common interest is on the wane.

"Civil religion," with Italy as a prime example, is characterized by "the attempt to govern the ethical, cultural and religious plurality of the country through the values of Catholicism, raised to the rank of civil religion." Full citizenship for non-Catholics as well as for Catholics is based on the assumption that Catholicism supplies the nation's cultural and ethical principles, and as long as the premise is accepted non-Catholics "enjoy religious freedom rights, although not religious equality rights." Ferrari sums up: "Governing diversity by stressing (Catholic) identity is the narrow and arduous path Italy is trying to follow."

Finally, France offers an example of *laïcité,* understood as a secular "cluster of universal and abstract values — liberty, equality, tolerance, etc." The French version of *laïcité* assumes that it "can include and reconcile the particular values of the religious, racial, ethnic, cultural, and political communities living in the country." It follows that national identity is conceived as a secular affair and that the state has the obligation to pursue *laïcité.* The increase of extensive inner-city clashes between groups of different ethnicities and persuasions reveals, however, the French difficulties with accommodating "the two driving forces that are changing the European landscape — the increasing plurality of religions and their growing public character." Ferrari continues: "The weakest point of the French pattern is the assumption that not only the State and its institutions but also society and politics have to be independent from particular traditions and conditions of life." And exactly this assumption is rejected by not at least Muslim immigrant communities.

The Turkish Republic, the Ecumenical Patriarchate, and the European Union

Laiklik

A Turkish version of *laïcité,* called *laiklik,* has regulated both the legal framework of the contemporary Turkish Republic and the mindset of a large sector of the Turkish society. Although different parts of the Turkish public have interpreted the word differently at different times, there is a common denominator, namely, the word's reference to the establishment in 1923 of Turkey as a secular republic after the collapse of the Ottoman Empire. Originally, and until very recent years, the Turkish form of *laïcité* referred to a system of religion-state relations based on having the state, its authorities, and the military actively promoting secularism and controlling religious practices and institutions. In the words of Patriarch Bartholomew, "Turkey is unique because there is a harmony between traditional Turkish Muslim values and secularism. As a matter of fact, Turkey is 'Islamic *and* secular' rather than 'Islamic, *but* secular.'"[29] Recent research argues, however, that the political landscape has changed so much since the moderate Islamist Justice and Development Party (the AK Party) won the 2002 and 2007 elections that the "character of religion-state relations in Turkey has changed from 'active secularism' to 'a more passive type.'" Some would even argue that the 2007 election de facto meant bridging the traditional gap between secularists and Islamicists.[30]

Within the focus and limits of this article a few notes on the changing ideas of *laïcité* will have to suffice. They will, inevitably, mirror my own reading of this utterly complex phenomenon. The Turkish version of *laïcité* is rooted in the pre-history of the Republic: the pro-Western ideas of its founder, Mustafa Kemal Atatürk, and the vision of the Young Turks,[31] not least the idea of the military's role as the defender of a secular state, made for the peculiar nature of *laïcité.* The foundational principles of the

29. Bartholomew, *In the World, Yet Not of the World,* 198.

30. Cf. James W. Warhola and Egemen B. Bezei, "Religion and State in Contemporary Turkey: Recent Developments in *Laiklik," Journal of Church and State* 52, no. 3 (2010): 427-453. I have quoted from pages 428 and 433.

31. The principle of *laiklik* was — together with, e.g., nationalism and republicanism — one of the "six arrows" with which the Republic was created. "Young Turks" refers to a modernizing, nationalistic movement at the end of the nineteenth and the beginning of the twentieth century favoring reforms of the Ottoman rule.

Turkish Republic as articulated by the Lausanne Treaty of 24 July 1924, guarantee the protection of life and liberty to all inhabitants of Turkey "without distinction of birth, nationality, language, race, or religion" and "free exercise, whether in public or private, of any creed, religion or belief, the observance of which shall not be incompatible with public order and good morals" (Article 38). The Treaty declares that all the inhabitants of Turkey, without distinction of religion, shall be equal before the law (Article 39), and it explicitly grants equal rights to non-Muslim minorities "to establish, manage, and control at their own expense, any charitable, religious, and social institutions, any schools and other establishments for instruction and education, with the right to use their own language and to exercise their religion freely therein" (Article 40). The history of the Turkish Republic reveals, however, that the religious freedom and the religion-state divide embedded in *laiklik* consistently has been understood as compatible with a strict state/military control over religion, either directly via the National Security Council, or indirectly via the Ministry for Religious Affairs.[32]

The dominant role of the Turkish military and the inherited demand for strict regulation of religious expressions have, however, waned as twenty-first-century Turkey experienced an emerging linkage between Islam and liberal modernity. Today a growing Muslim middle class

> repositions Islam vis-à-vis global modernity and world cultural principles such as universal rights, international law and institutions, individuation, multiculturalism, liberalism, the free market, and democracy. This repositioning is pervasive among the areas of theology and faith (*din* [religion]); everyday life, economics, and lifestyles (*dunya* [world]); and politics and political participation (*deylet* [state]) . . . This reframing, nonetheless, is not secularization . . . (but submitted) to an "objective truth" and an "objective separation" between *halal* [permissible] and *haram* [impermissible].[33]

32. According to Warhola and Bezei, "Religion and State in Contemporary Turkey," the military's involvement in upholding *laiklik* against Islamist movements was a determining factor in the coups of 1960, 1971, 1980, and in the 1997 ultimatum calling for the resignation of the government. "The legacy of the Western-oriented Young Turks, the effective military rule during the war of Independence 1919-1922, the legacy of Atatürk's 'six arrows' . . . , and the cultural fusion of military and religious symbols and expressions make for a profoundly complex tapestry in which *laiklik* works out in concrete practice" (428).

33. Neslihan Cevik, "The Theological Roots of Liberalism in Turkey: 'Muslimism' from Islamic Fashion to Foreign Policy," *The Hedgehog Review* 13, no. 2 (Summer 2011).

The attitude is neither state-centered nor community-centered, but an indicator of an emerging individual-centered Islam in which faith is a personal choice.

In a 2009 interview with CBS's *60 Minutes*,[34] Patriarch Bartholomew commented on the history and actual practice of Turkish religion-state relations. He mentioned the confiscation of Christian property: church buildings, monasteries, and schools. Because Turkey does not recognize the church as a juridical person, it takes a cumbersome establishment of independent funds to own property, including church buildings. The transcript of the interview does not name any specific church building, but like a number of other churches in Istanbul, both the Chora Church (*Chóra*, Greek for "outside the city; in the fields"), with its unsurpassed Byzantine mosaics, and the Hagia Sophia, for centuries the greatest church building in the world, function as museums.[35] Most recently, on 28 August 2011, Turkish Prime Minister Recep Tayyip Erdogan promised a gathering of 161 religious minority associations that a significant number of confiscated properties, if claimed within a year, would be returned to religious minorities. The promise reveals a changed attitude towards religious minorities; however, if returned to the Ecumenical Patriarchate, Orthodox Christians could not fill all these buildings. Massacres and deportations during World War I, the population exchange between Greece and Turkey in 1923, the emigration of 1932 caused by commercial restrictions, a severe taxation of non-Muslims in 1932, and a 1955 persecution of Christians in Istanbul have severely diminished the Greek population in Turkey to between three and four thousand.[36]

Although the Copenhagen criteria for membership in the European Union (1993) require stable institutions guaranteeing democracy, the rule of law, human rights, and protection of minorities (in Turkey "minorities" are defined also on the basis of religion), the CBS interview does not hide the Patriarch's assessment that Turkey provides only second-class citizenship to Orthodox Christians: ". . . we don't feel that we enjoy our full rights

---

34. CBS News, www.cbsnews.com/stories/2009/12/17/60minutes/main5990390.shtml. Accessed 27 December 2010.

35. Cf. Rüstem Aslan, Stephan W. E. Blum, and Frank Schweizer, *Byzanz — Konstantinopel — Istanbul* (Mainz: Wissenschaftliche Buchgessellschaft, 2010). During his tenure the Patriarch has restored the church buildings and charitable centers that belong to the Orthodox Church.

36. Cf. Robert Ellis, advisor to the Turkey Assessment Group of the European Parliament, *Kr. Dagblad,* 12 November 2010 (in Danish).

as Turkish citizens." He complains of not receiving an answer when he submits concrete problems to the authorities, but when asked why he does not move the Patriarchate to Greece, he refers to its pre-Islamic history in Constantinople, saying, "Our mission is here as it has been for seventeen entire centuries . . . and I wonder why the authorities of our country do not respect this history." "We do believe in miracles" was the terse reply when the reporter hinted at possible fears that the Christian community might be wiped out.

A year earlier, in a 2008 interview, Patriarch Bartholomew specified some of his grievances.[37] The list is long, headed by the closure in 1971 of the Orthodox school of theology on the island of Halki, off Istanbul. The closure was a consequence of a ban on private higher education, and the result has been a threat to the lifeline of the Orthodox Church, because Turkish law prescribes Turkish citizenship for priests and, *a fortiori,* for the Ecumenical Patriarch. Another of the Patriarch's complaints about government control of the Orthodox Church addresses the Turkish government's understanding of the status of Patriarch as a local bishop, and the consequent denial — in the summer of 2007 — of any legal recognition of the Patriarch as the head of a worldwide communion of Orthodox churches. "But," Patriarch Bartholomew continues, "the secular attitudes of Turkey are our main problem. We have fewer problems with most of the religious Muslims we meet in the corridors of the state than with the strong secularists and the right-wing nationalists who do not want to have any Christian minorities in the country."

Some reforms of state-religion relationships have been adopted, the Patriarch acknowledges, but the implementation has been slow. He then returns to his hope for Turkey's speedy entry into the European Union, and shares his conviction that EU membership will benefit the Turkish population:

> We shall gain prosperity, stability and democracy . . . and the minorities will fare better, if Turkey will submit to the European norms. Today we have the freedom to worship, to sing and have the church bells sound, but that is not enough. We still lack full religious freedom and encounter some discrimination because of our faith. Usually I say that when religion and state is separated in a secular republic like Turkey, how can the state then encroach on minorities, just because they are Christians?

---

37. *Kr. Dagblad,* 7 March 2008 (in Danish).

Laïcité with a New Makeup

From 1999 onwards, especially since the AK Party took over the government in 2002, the civil influence on Turkish politics has gained weight while, correspondingly, the role of the military has declined. The National Security Council has been placed under civilian authority, and the military and the civilian authorities have effectively joined efforts to modernize Turkey with the intent to comply with the European Union's legal, political, and economic prescriptions for accepting the Republic as a (full) member of the community. In spite of loudly touted misgivings, the progress reports of the European Commission do acknowledge Turkish attempts to have its laws and political system conform to "European norms."[38] Not least the presidential election in 2007 changed the secularity of the Turkish Republic by placing the religiously oriented AK Party's candidate, Abdullah Gül, as the head of "a secular republic." A 2009 description of the shifts in the religion-state relations runs as follows: "[Research] asserts that while the Islamic segment is becoming secular on its own, the secular segment is also democratizing. These are the dominant attitudes of the majority." Although the assessment operates with a too simplistic divide between Islamic faith and a secular state, it is correct in stating, "Rigid Islamic and secular attitudes constitute the minority."[39]

The historical basis for a shift in the interpretation of *laiklik* must be found in the profound *social changes* that have created an urban business class demanding space for social and commercial networking free of state control; in the *cultural changes* that have debunked the traditional Islamic preference for a homogeneous unity of religion and state; and in the *religious changes* that in the interest of individual faith allow for a variety of Islamic movements and minorities.[40] A summary drawn up by Warhola and Bezei is worth quoting:

> Turkey's secular state was clearly of the "active secular" type for nearly the history of the Republic, as evidenced by strict control of religious

38. Cf. Ali Resul Usul, *Democracy in Turkey* (New York: Routledge, 2011). The European Commission for Democracy through Law (referred to as the Venice Commission) used the expression "European norms" in its evaluation (March 2010) of the legal status of religious minorities in Turkey: www.venic.coe.int/docs/2010.

39. Quoted in Warhola and Bezei, "Religion and State in Contemporary Turkey," 440.

40. On the influential Gülen movement and its combination of moderate, traditional Islam and a commitment to education on a global scale, cf. Tobias Specker, "Vertraue auf Gott und sie fleissig," *Herder Korrespondenz* 2 (2011): 96-101.

leadership, education, formal recognition (or lack thereof) of religious communities, and in general a state-controlled political climate in terms of the role of religion in the public sphere . . . , [but] *laiklik* has been slowly, but significantly shifting in the direction of a "passive secular" type of state-religion relation.[41]

Patriarch Bartholomew speaks publicly about being pleased with these developments. An interview conducted on 17 November 2010 in Istanbul[42] deals explicitly with the liturgy he was able to celebrate on the Feast of the Dormition of Mary (15 August 2010) in the Soumela Monastery close to Trabzon on the coast of the Black Sea. The city had become infamous in recent years because of murders of Christian clergy there, and the permission to celebrate in the monastery was valid only once a year. His All Holiness nevertheless evaluates this opening, and the parallel opening up for an Armenian liturgy once a year in the Church of the Holy Cross on an island in Lake Van, as a positive change in Turkish attitudes. He says,

> What happened at Panagia Soumela proved that the place [which is officially a museum] can also once a year serve as a place of worship . . . This is something beneficial for all. The Turkish state understands that we are not a threat but, on the contrary, that we love and work for the good of our country. Beyond the material benefits for the country resulting from the pilgrims, such actions are evidence that respect of religious freedom is growing in Turkey. This is a matter of principles and values in relation to basic human rights.

He refers to the European Court of Human Rights and its ruling of 15 June 2010 that the confiscated orphanage on the island of Büyükada/Prinkipos in the Sea of Marmara should be returned to the Patriarchate, and he mentions his optimistic belief that the issue of the Halki seminary will be solved.

Asked about his attitude to the Turkish government's approach to minorities, the Patriarch does not balk at the political question, but reiterates,

> It is no secret that we are really glad about these steps of the Turkish government. We support this approach. We hope that it will continue in

41. Warhola and Bezei, "Religion and State in Contemporary Turkey," 452-453.

42. Cf. the transcript on www.johnsanidopoulos.com/2010/11/ecumenical-patriarch-speaks-with.html. Accessed 3 January 2011.

the future. Furthermore . . . we believe that such negotiations will render Turkey even more democratic as a country, which is precisely the reason we are supporting Turkey's full EU membership.

The statement echoes the Patriarch's address to the Plenary Assembly of the European Parliament in 2008 that emphasized the importance of "the European Project" for "the need to embrace the fullness of shared presence within the human ecosphere" and consequently Europe's obligation to bring Turkey into its Project and Turkey's obligation "to foster inter-cultural dialogue and tolerance in order to be accepted into the European Project."[43]

Dragging Feet: Turning Eastward and Inward

There is no doubt that the efforts to gain membership in the EU have been a decisive force in the reforms of Turkey's legal system and the concomitant loosening of state control with the exercise of religious Human Rights. "Between 1999 and 2007, 'Compliance with the European standard' regarding democracy and human rights became the keywords referred to by the Turkish state and the political elite in order to legitimize significant legal and political changes."[44] The implemented transformations of the Turkish society made it possible for the German president to make a speech in October 2010 before the Grand National Assembly of Turkey that included the following lines:

[With the reforms over the last few decades and especially in recent years] Turkey is taking more steps towards European standards . . . Both of our countries have long been members of the Council of Europe. For many years, we have been bound by the principles of human rights, democracy and the rule of law, as laid down in the European Convention

43. www.patriarchate.org/documents/plenary08. Accessed 19 February 2011.

44. Usul, *Democracy in Turkey,* 140. The EU declared Turkey an official candidate at the Helsinki Summit in 1999. The accession negotiations began in 2006. References to the EU Commission's progress reports (1999 to 2007), the Accession Partnership documents, the Turkish National Programmes, the 2001 and 2004 constitutional amendments, and the establishment of human rights organizations within the state apparatus are found on pages 72-142. Usul's list (141) of the most significant reforms begins with the transformation of the National Security Council and includes easing non-Muslim minorities' rights to purchase tangible assets.

on Human Rights. This includes the protection of minorities as well as religious and cultural pluralism . . . [We] expect Christians in Islamic countries to enjoy the . . . right to openly live their faith, educate their own clergy and build churches . . . Here in Turkey, there is a long tradition of Christianity. There is no doubt that Christianity is part of Turkey . . . After all, religious freedom is part of our understanding of Europe as a community of shared values.[45]

The German president's stance may be compared to the Ecumenical Patriarch's message to a Euroconference in Florence in 2001: "[F]or more than fifteen hundred years the Orthodox faith has preached love, reconciliation, and mutual understanding, irrespective of personal background, race or gender. Our vision is that the new Europe must be based on these Christian values, according to which government, civil society, and religion are partners and not rivals . . ."[46]

These statements take us back to "Europe as an idea" as the founding principle of European identity, once envisioned with Turkey as a unifying "other" and now envisioned as a shared Turkish-EU identity. But is such an identity desirable? In February 2011 the EU Secretaries of State encountered serious difficulties with finding a common vocabulary for a condemnation of recent persecutions of Christians in the Middle East, and the disagreement shows the mounting "fear of Muslims" that has fed a return to the rhetoric of the Mantua Congress and its questioning of the "Europeanness" of Turkey. Prejudices concerning the religious, cultural, and political characteristics of Turkish society have fueled opposition to "multiculturalism." In the fall of 2010 the German chancellor declared multiculturalism a total fiasco, and in the early spring of 2011 the British prime minister repeated that multiculturalism had failed. Domestic politics currently top the political and economic agenda of the Western European countries, and on the Turkish side the public support for the EU is in decline. A number of lawmakers and sections of the population have given up on the dream of Europe.[47] The access to EU membership seems to them to be blocked by

---

45. English version available at www.bundespraesident.de/en/-5669130/Speech-by-Christian-Wulff. Accessed 17 February 2010.

46. Bartholomew, *In the World, Yet Not of the World*, 122.

47. Orhan Pamuk, "The Fading Dream of Europe," *New York Review of Books*, 20 February 2011, 20. For a critical assessment of the arguments against Turkey's membership in the EU, see Ingmar Karlsson, "Turkey's Historical, Cultural and Religious Heritage: An Asset to the European Union?" in *European and Turkish Voices In Favour and Against Turkish Ac-*

major players like Germany and France and the process deadlocked by a never-ending insertion of ever new conditions for Turkey's joining the European "we." As reported by the *New York Times Magazine,* U.S. Defense Secretary Robert Gates has suggested that "if there is anything to the notion that Turkey is, if you will, moving eastward, [it is the result of having been] pushed by some in Europe refusing to give Turkey the sort of organic link to the West that Turkey sought."[48]

It is futile to prophesy on the shape of future religion-state relationships, but one need not speculate on the current Turkish version of *laiklik.* If Turkey enjoyed full-fledged religious freedom, no church authority would have to seek permission from secular authorities to celebrate the liturgy. The repeated European demands to recognize communities like the Ecumenical Patriarchate and the Chief Rabbinate as "juridical persons" would have been met, as would the demands enumerated in detail in March 2010 by the European Commission for Democracy through Law (usually named the Venice Commission).[49]

But the EU drags its feet, and Prime Minister Erdogan has warned that ties to the EU might be broken if Cyprus is included in the rotating leadership of the EU. In 2012, Turkish diplomacy has made more than one about-face. It tried but failed in effectively cultivating a principle of "zero problems toward neighbors" (including Armenia, Iran, Syria, and Israel), and in the aftermath of the "Arab Spring" the Ecumenical Patriarchate could find itself in a context that may be described as a new nationalist version of Turkey as the heir of Ottoman greatness and the unprecedented example of an Islamic democracy and the first secular republic of the Islamic world.[50]

---

cession to the European Union, ed. Christiana Timmerman, Dirk Rochtus, and Sara Mels (Brussels: Peter Lang, 2008). On domestic politics, in Turkey and in EU member states, as decisive for the outcome of the accession processes, see Esra LaGro and Knud Erik Jørgensen, eds., *Turkey and the European Union: Prospects for a Difficult Encounter* (New York: Palgrave Macmillan, 2007).

48. Quoted from James Traub, "Turkey's Rules," *New York Times Magazine,* 23 January 2011, 35.

49. In addition to demanding recognition of the Ecumenical Patriarchate as a "juridical person," the Parliamentary Assembly of the Council of Europe demanded on 17 January 2010 that Turkey recognize the Patriarchate's rights to use the adjective "ecumenical" and gave instant attention to solving the problems related to both the Halki seminary and the work permits for non-Turkish clergy. The Venice Commission's list of desired Turkish changes of state-religion relationships is accessible at www.venice.coe.int/docs/2010.

50. Cf. Stephen Kinzer, "Triumphant Turkey?" *New York Review of Books,* 18 August 2011, 37-40.

Speaking to journalists ahead of a visit to Armenia in April 2011, Turkish President Abdullah Gül emphasized that the future Turkey would be a country with influence and would make a great contribution to the EU, but he also warned that the Turkish people might reject EU membership, like Norway did. Naming the obstacles to Turkish membership unjust, he pointed to Turkey's compliance with the agreements and explicitly mentioned that "people of different faith shouldn't be ignored or isolated."[51] At the fourteenth Eurasian Economic Summit, 13-15 April 2011, in Istanbul, Patriarch Bartholomew also underlined the importance of Turkey's role in the globalizing world and added, "Western and secular people have depicted religion as the sole factor responsible for the problems of the world. But religion is not the factor that should be accused," he said. It is, on the contrary, "an important dynamic in the world's transformation."[52] Whether the EU will agree that "religion is no source of tension," as the Turkish reporting from the Patriarch's summit address put it, is an open question. The century-old quest for "the soul of Europe" is far from over.

51. www.news.az/articles/turkey/35423. Accessed 4 May 2011.
52. *Daily News* (Istanbul), 15 April 2011.

CHAPTER 2

Bartholomew as a Leader in the Orthodox Church

Peter C. Bouteneff

When it came to addressing Ecumenical Patriarch Bartholomew's leadership of the Orthodox Church, it may seem curious to some — as it did to me — that the editor of this volume did not choose someone from the Patriarch's inner circle, nor even from the See of Constantinople or its dioceses in Europe or in the Americas, but an apolitical layman, and furthermore someone from the Orthodox Church in America, a church whose relationship with the Ecumenical Patriarchate has been strained over the question of its autocephaly since 1970. Perhaps this was done to signal that readers could expect a "realistic" (rather than overly rosy) assessment of the Patriarch's leadership in the Orthodox Church. Whether he knew it or not, the editor chose someone who — while not immune to frustrations over the autocephaly question — stands in deep esteem of the vision and achievements of the present Patriarch. My data on him is gleaned from what he has said and done, as well as from personal encounters I have enjoyed with him through my involvement in intra-Orthodox and inter-Christian affairs. I trust that the esteem, and indeed the love that I have for the Patriarch will help rather than hinder in producing a potently affirmative yet not entirely uncritical assessment of his leadership of the Orthodox Church. This assessment will not pretend to be comprehensive nor can it address all areas of his leadership of the Church. I seek here to present a series of reflections on certain key areas of his work that I see as emblematic of his priorities and the character of his tenure thus far, within the particular landscape of contemporary Orthodoxy — something I will also attempt to describe, where relevant.

Peter C. Bouteneff

External Witness and Its Internal Significance

While this volume is predominantly given over to the Patriarch's activity in and effect upon the non-Orthodox world, it would be a mistake to consider his external witness as distinct from his effect upon the thought and life of the Orthodox Church. Whatever he has said and done in the "outside" context has important implications for the Orthodox Church itself as a testimony to the vision and the priorities of the *primus inter pares* of the Orthodox Church's leaders. To begin with, then, I would highlight two areas of this so-called "witness to the outside world" as being of monumental importance for the Orthodox: his commitment to inter-Christian relationships, and his promotion of environmental issues. I will also here discuss briefly his witness within the strained relationship between the Patriarchate and the Turkish state.

Inter-Christian Relationships

It is impossible to appreciate the importance of the Patriarch's stance on ecumenical relationships without establishing something of the context of contemporary Orthodox vis-à-vis non-Orthodox Christians. Although all but two of the canonical Orthodox churches are full members of the WCC, and although pan-Orthodox meetings have formally endorsed ecumenical participation as part of the Church's mission,[1] the Orthodox have had a stormy and uneven experience with ecumenism since its modern origins. All the Christian churches today have large or small pockets of resistance to relationships with other Christians, and there are certainly large swaths of Christianity who elect not to participate in local or especially global ecumenical institutions, most notably the World Council of Churches. Within global expressions of Christianity, the Orthodox Church presents a particularly volatile and internally varied case.

To begin with, there are literally scores of small churches that are separated from the canonical Orthodox Church over the interrelated issues of ecumenism and the decision to follow the "New" (Gregorian, or Revised

---

1. See the Third Panorthodox Preconciliar Conference, Chambésy, 1986, especially Section III. Available online at http://www.oikoumene.org/en/resources/documents/wcc-programmes/ecumenical-movement-in-the-21st-century/member-churches/special-commission-on-participation-of-the-orthodox-churches/first-plenary-meeting-documents-december-1999.

Julian) Calendar. These each have their own history, their own raisons d'être, and complex sets of interrelationships: many are out of communion not only with the canonical Orthodox Church but with each other as well. However, partly owing to the internet, they have been able to exert a more or less univocal influence against "ecumenism." That influence has served both to galvanize their own stance of "resistance" as well as to play upon anti-ecumenical, xenophobic, and fundamentalistic tendencies within sectors of the canonical churches. This means that among the faithful as well as among clergy and hierarchy one may find loud voices that insist upon the cessation of all inter-Christian dialogue and cooperation and that accuse those (including the Patriarch) who participate in dialogues and in the ecumenical institutions of heresy. In a phenomenon that is sometimes though not always related, there are powerful sub-currents in the Orthodox churches espousing sectarian, anti-Semitic, and Masonic conspiracy theories. Again, as a random perusal of "Orthodox" websites will quickly attest, Orthodoxy today presents a volatile and varied landscape.

The anti-ecumenical literature emanating both from without as well as from within the canonical churches has frequently targeted Patriarch Bartholomew directly. Yet just as his positions have prompted increasingly extreme anti-ecumenical reactions, the attacks on the Patriarch have elicited an unequivocal and ever-strengthening commitment from him to pursue dialogue with other churches and to support ecumenical institutions.

One recent anti-ecumenical proclamation implicates hierarchs (including patriarchs), monastics, clergy, and laypersons, charging that, by engaging in "common prayers, with exchanges of visits, with pastoral collaborations" they are "essentially placing themselves outside the Church."[2] This document emerging from the (canonical) Church of Greece in April 2009 and entitled "A Confession of Faith against Ecumenism" also criticizes the 1920 encyclical of the Ecumenical Patriarchate "Unto the Churches of Christ Everywhere," and makes numerous sweeping statements about "Papism" and Protestantism. It would be easy to ignore such a document or to consign it to the realm of sociology rather than to ecclesiastical and theological reflection. However, it has amassed a considerable number of signatories who include hierarchs and other persons of influence in the Church.

Patriarch Bartholomew publicly signaled his reaction to the document

2. This document is available online at http://www.impantokratoros.gr/FA9AF77F .en.aspx.

with a response that, although forceful, was of a piece with his consistent commitment to genuine, sober, and theologically attentive relationships with non-Orthodox Christians and the ecumenical institutions. It is significant that this response was delivered as an encyclical on the Sunday of Orthodoxy — also known as "The Triumph of Orthodoxy," a day on which the Orthodox Church celebrates the strict dogmatic continuity of her faith with that of the apostles, in part through the chanting of anathemas against heretical views. In other words, it is a day of celebrating the Orthodox Church and her true faith, in contradistinction to heresy.

The Patriarchal encyclical[3] affirms the pan-Orthodox nature of ecumenical involvement and commitment, and the seriousness of the God-given command to pursue unity among divided Christians. The Patriarch is especially strong on this latter point, asserting that to "remain indifferent about the unity of all Christians . . . would constitute criminal betrayal and transgression of His divine commandment."[4] Having chided the anti-ecumenical "zealots" for fomenting distrust through the distortion of facts and through demagoguery, he exhorts the faithful,

> Beloved children in the Lord, Orthodoxy has no need of either fanaticism or bigotry to protect itself. Whoever believes that Orthodoxy has the truth does not fear dialogue, because truth has never been endangered by dialogue. By contrast, when in our day all people strive to resolve their differences through dialogue, Orthodoxy cannot proceed with intolerance and extremism.[5]

The people of the Church are left with no doubt about where the Ecumenical Patriarch stands on the matter of inter-Christian dialogue, the goal of unity, as well as the corrosive role played by "fanaticism," "bigotry," "intolerance," and "extremism." This is a crucial witness within a contemporary Orthodoxy that, even as it justly seeks to assert its uniqueness and its fidelity to the One Apostolic Faith, is prone to doing so through a harmful zealotry.

Of course, not all critics of ecumenical involvement are equally seditious or malicious, and there are valid theological concerns surrounding

---

3. See John Chryssavgis and Rowan Williams, eds., *Speaking the Truth in Love: Theological and Spiritual Exhortations of Ecumenical Patriarch Bartholomew* (New York: Fordham University Press, 2011), 193-196.

4. Chryssavgis and Williams, *Speaking the Truth in Love*, 194.

5. Chryssavgis and Williams, *Speaking the Truth in Love*, 196.

ecumenism that require a response. The Patriarch does not seem to feel that these are his responsibility: as bearers of the theological weight of ecumenism he has enlisted people who are regarded within and outside Orthodoxy as being among the best theologians of our era — should it not be they who argue for the theological bases of ecumenical engagement? Furthermore, are there not clear guidelines for ecumenical involvement?[6] Perhaps, too, he senses that the "zealot" voices are not sincerely interested in a serious theological conversation about inter-Christian dialogue and its various contexts: their motivations and priorities lie elsewhere.

He may be correct on this assumption: the stance of "resistance" and "prophetic witness" of the people against an allegedly wrong-minded patriarch has a sainted history in the Church's life, but it has also shown itself to be a highly seductive stance wherein anyone can portray oneself and one's cohorts as the last righteous remnant. This identity and status are not yielded easily. On the other hand, there are statements emanating from the Patriarch — perhaps especially those within a Roman Catholic context — that seem to push the boundaries of a dogmatic ecclesiology, perhaps even challenging some of the commonly understood principles of Orthodox ecumenical involvement. Regularly addressing the Pope of Rome as "elder brother," listing him first in the diptychs at ecumenical doxologies, goes beyond the contested language of "sister churches" that has floated in and out of usage between the Orthodox and Roman Catholic churches for centuries.[7] His critics on this score tend to ignore the fact that the overwhelmingly gracious tones of his language toward the Pope are offset by sharp theological criticism of the papacy.[8] It might still be argued that the Patriarch owes people a response to questions about such language. Yet again, especially because of the level and the tone of much of the criticism leveled against him, he leaves this response to others. He is too busy engaging in the hard work of nurturing relationships within the hugely intricate inter-Christian landscape.

That this patriarch so strenuously and consistently advocates dia-

6. See, e.g., the Ecumenical Guidelines for the Standing Conference of the Canonical Orthodox Bishops in the Americas, available online at http://www.scoba.us/resources/ecumenical_guidelines.html.

7. See most recently Will Cohen, "The Concept of 'Sister Churches' in the Orthodox-Catholic Relations in the 12th and 21st Centuries," *St. Vladimir's Theological Quarterly* 53 (2009): 375-406.

8. See Olivier Clément, *Conversations with Ecumenical Patriarch Bartholomew I*, trans. Paul Meyendorff (Crestwood, NY: St. Vladimir's Seminary Press, 1997), 189.

logue, is committed to Christian unity in the apostolic faith, understands Orthodoxy to be the true faith and the Orthodox Church to be the Church, and yet acknowledges the need for repentance for sins committed in the name of the Church during its history, and that he clearly confronts fanaticism and anti-ecumenical hysteria within the Church's own ranks, is a witness of inestimable significance. In today's Orthodox world, marked as it is by pockets of sectarianism and fundamentalism, his stance is as vital as it is courageous.

The Environment

The well-known stance of the "Green Patriarch" on the environment has met with a variety of reactions. To some he is a hero; to others, at minimum a sellout to vague or "liberal" causes. From the onset of his efforts to bring attention to the state of the natural world, there were those who felt this a harmless but finally "uncostly" stance. Everyone loves the natural world. No one really has to go out on a limb to show that the created cosmos is a good thing, and that it is in danger. It is a neat way to divert attention from ecclesiastical struggles.

Recent years have proved this appraisal drastically wrong. Perhaps especially in America, the environment is a deeply politicized topic, as the debate over climate change has shown. The political right tends to claim environmental crises to be hoaxes or exaggerations, leaving it to the political left to argue for their reality. Business interests are never far removed from the debate. And Orthodox Christians, together with others, are liable to be caught up in the political confusion, making conclusions about the environment on the basis of their own right- or left-leaning tendencies, rather than on the basis of the Church's explicit teaching and implicit understanding.

In such a context the Patriarch's role is of paramount importance. Although some Orthodox try to cast his environmental priorities as an accommodation to the political left, such a view ignores what the Patriarch is actually saying and doing. For he shows that love and care for the created world, and a consistently responsible treatment of it, emanate not from any political or economic impulse but rather entirely from the Church's theological tradition. By the late twentieth century, modern Orthodox theology had already provided foundations for such a stance by consistently emphasizing the goodness of the created world, in distinction from either a Manichaean dualism or an undue pessimism emanating from other

Christian quarters. The sacramental theology (for decades associated primarily with Fr. Alexander Schmemann)[9] had likewise begun to awaken Orthodox and non-Orthodox to the Eucharistic significance of the created world. Studies in Christian anthropology, perhaps especially through an awakened interest in the writings of St. Maximus the Confessor, highlighted also the role of the human person in mediating between the created cosmos and the uncreated God.

Patriarch Bartholomew has taken all of this further in several directions. He has engaged collaboratively with theologians such as Dr. John Chryssavgis to help articulate a wide-ranging theology grounded in the writings of the Church Fathers, taking note also of their ascetical writings, since asceticism primarily involves the pursuit of right *relationships* — between human beings and their creator, each other, and the created world. He has worked with scientists and sociologists in organizing colloquia fostering environmental consciousness-raising as well as policy change. The importance of these priorities and actions for the wider world is obvious, is documented elsewhere in this volume, and has been rightly celebrated. But here again, the witness *within* the Orthodox world is less well recognized. For Orthodox Christians to behold an Ecumenical Patriarch who is so attuned — in both a holistic and a creative fashion — to society and theology speaks volumes about the relevance of their own theological and ascetical tradition and the ways in which it transcends political rhetoric.

Church and State: Constantinople and Istanbul

The location of the Patriarchate of Constantinople in modern-day Istanbul and the relationship between the Patriarchate and the Turkish state constitute a further set of issues that bridge Patriarch Bartholomew's external and internal witness.[10] Constantinople has been the seat of an archiepiscopal see since the fourth century; its ruling hierarch has had the title of "Ecumenical Patriarch" since the sixth.[11] Maintaining this status, in this geo-

9. See especially *For the Life of the World: Sacraments and Orthodoxy,* 2d ed. (Crestwood, NY: St. Vladimir's Seminary Press, 1973).

10. A very useful collection of his public addresses in Turkish contexts can be found in *In the World, Yet Not of the World: Social and Global Initiatives of Ecumenical Patriarch Bartholomew,* ed. John Chryssavgis (New York: Fordham University Press, 2010), 195-221.

11. The term "Ecumenical Patriarch" (and the concomitant idea that the see, and not just its primate, is "ecumenical" in nature) is harder to trace and is probably modern in its origins.

graphical location, has been an unceasing struggle since the fall of Constantinople to the Ottomans in 1453. The ensuing five and a half centuries have seen the Patriarch living under governments that have been sometimes more and sometimes less accommodating, but never according the Church complete freedom.

The embattled and dwindling state of today's Greek community in Turkey is well known. The tragic Greek-Turkish population exchange of 1924 displaced 2 million people, 1.5 million of whom were Asia-Minor Greeks. Another 150,000 Greeks fled government-sponsored anti-Greek violence in 1955. At the beginning of the twentieth century, Greeks made up a third of Constantinople's population of 1 million people. At the beginning of the twenty-first, there may be 2,000 Greeks remaining in a city of 15 million. Although contemporary Turkey is technically a secular state, its population is over 99% Muslim. Orthodox Christians in Turkey have been identified as one of the world's most vulnerable religious communities, threatened with extinction within a decade.[12] In the face of these dire factors, added to which are strained relations with the contemporary government and periodic threats — and occasional acts — of violence to the Patriarch and the Patriarchate, some have called for the relocation of the Patriarchate of Constantinople outside of Turkey. Yet decamping from its current and historical location has never been seen as a realistic option by sitting patriarchs, Bartholomew included.

During a recent televised interview, Patriarch Bartholomew reaffirmed his stance on the importance of remaining in Istanbul. That city, he said, is "the continuation of Jerusalem, and for us it is equally a holy and sacred land."[13] He spoke of the patriarchate's sojourn there in terms of suffering and crucifixion. "We love our country, we are born here, we want to die here. Our mission is here, as it has been for seventeen centuries." He likewise voiced deep frustrations at his multiple attempts to attain greater freedom and recognition for the Ecumenical Patriarchate from the Turkish government, none of which, he said, have met with success. (The state recognizes the patriarch to be the spiritual leader of the Greek Orthodox residents of Istanbul, and does not accord to him any transnational role.)

In one of the harsher blows to the Patriarchate and to worldwide Ortho-

---

12. See the report "Minority Religious Communities at Risk" by the nondenominational First Freedom Center, available online at http://www.firstfreedom.org/index.html. See especially pages 8-9.

13. Televised interview on CBS's *60 Minutes*, 20 December 2009.

doxy, the Theological School of Halki, founded in 1844 as the main theological educational training facility for clergy and theologians of the Constantinopolitan See, was closed in 1974 and remains in an enforced state of disuse. The movement to reopen the school has been one of the Patriarch's main causes during his numerous national and international state visits. This campaign has been supported at the highest level through visits by U.S. President Bill Clinton, through resolutions passed by the U.S. Congress, and through the backing of the European Union. Current U.S. President Barack Obama has highlighted the cause during a speech to the Turkish Parliament in April 2009.[14] The groundswell of international support is testimony both to the increasing and unprecedented boldness as well as the effectiveness of Patriarch Bartholomew's witness to the international community. One can only react with astonishment that his pleas, together with those of the international community, have gone unheeded. The witness of the Patriarchate of Constantinople in Istanbul continues to be a kenotic one.

Intra-Orthodox Leadership

Patriarch Bartholomew's leadership of the Orthodox Church as *primus inter pares* of the heads of the local autocephalous churches is marked in a wide variety of ways. I would like to explore a selection of them through the lens of the ministry of primacy, and how it has been viewed and exercised under Patriarch Bartholomew's headship.

The Ministry of Primacy

The government and oversight of the Christian Church since its inception have been founded on a deliberate but delicate interweaving of conciliarity and primacy. This relationship looks to the archetypal relationship of the three Trinitarian Persons as articulated during the early Christian centuries. For even within the Trinity itself there is a *taxis* or order: the Father is the sole source of, and yet never exists or acts without, his coeternal Son and Spirit.

Primacy and conciliarity are emblematic of the relationships within

---

14. Available online at http://www.america.gov/st/texttrans-english/2009/April/20090406112929eaifaso.5201685.html.

and between the local autocephalous Orthodox churches in ways that are modeled to varying extents on the Trinitarian pattern. Yet looking at the churches today, one could almost come away feeling that the ineffable Trinitarian mystery is more universally understood and agreed upon than that of ecclesiastical primacy, particularly as it pertains to the exact nature and implications of the primacy of the Ecumenical Patriarch. The relationship between conciliarity and primacy in the ecclesiastical sphere was codified in the Apostolic Canons (notably the 34th) formally recognized in A.D. 692.[15] The 28th canon of the Council of Chalcedon, which gives jurisdiction to Constantinople over "the barbarian lands," is understood in a greater variety of ways.[16]

No one denies the reality of primacy among the churches and the unique primatial role of the Patriarch of Constantinople. Yet history has seen different modes of the exercise of this primacy and different understandings of what constitutes "the barbarian lands"; moreover, the different local churches today testify to a certain variety of interpretations, from maximal to minimal, of the Constantinopolitan primacy.

Several episodes have emerged during Patriarch Bartholomew's tenure that have highlighted these different interpretations. In 1996 the Patriarch, responding to the urgent plea of the "Estonian Church in Exile," granted it recognition and reactivated an autonomy that Constantinople had given it in 1923. This was interpreted by Moscow as an act of interference upon its ancient canonical territory. A similar controversy has continued to evolve within the complex ecclesiastical landscape of Ukraine, which likewise emanates from different perceptions of the "reach" of Constantinopolitan primacy. In these and other cases, Patriarch Bartholomew has affirmed a robust interpretation of that primacy.

More broadly, the Orthodox Church today, facing challenges to its unity and identity in a demographically and politically evolving landscape, has embodied conflicting demands on its Ecumenical Patriarch. On the one hand, it has stood in need of a clear and centralized focus of leadership, a central figure, a head — let us admit it: a figure in some ways like a Pope, who speaks for and represents his entire church. On the other hand, Orthodox ecclesiastical governance has often rightly been defined in sharp

---

15. See P.-P. Joanou, *Discipline Général Antique*, vol. 1, pt. 2 (Rome: Commissione per la Redazione del Codice di Diritto Canonico Orientale, 1962), especially Apostolic Canon 34.

16. See Norman P. Tanner, S.J., ed., *Decrees of the Ecumenical Councils*, vol. 1 (Washington, DC: Georgetown University Press, 1990), 99-100.

distinction from the Roman papacy, especially in its post–Vatican I under-standing, where the Bishop of Rome has the power to elect or depose any bishop anywhere in the world, and to speak or teach authoritatively and infallibly "from himself and not from the consensus of the Church."[17]

Patriarch Bartholomew's exercise of leadership, as seen, for example, in the cases of Estonia and Ukraine, has been subjected to charges of "papal" governance. While these accusations are surely far-fetched, less exaggerated ecclesiological tensions among the Orthodox churches have emerged, often through disputes in ecumenical contexts. Does Orthodox church identity rely on communion with the See of Constantinople, or on the mutual inter-communion of the Orthodox churches? Each position has been argued by different hierarch theologians. The former has elicited uncomfortable com-parisons to the Roman model of communion with the Papal See; the latter has been seen as compromising a proper dynamic of primacy.

These tensions are indicative of a genuine and persistent impasse among the churches with regard to their understanding of primacy. From his enthronement in 1991 onward, the Patriarch has expressed his commit-ment to exercise his primacy in canonical and pastoral adherence to the principles of conciliarity.[18] His understanding of the primacy-conciliarity balance, and that of other Orthodox churches, is central with regard to an-other crucial issue that has faced the Orthodox world in the modern era, and which has been a major area of Patriarch Bartholomew's leadership: Orthodoxy outside its historical sees, or Orthodoxy in the "diaspora."

Orthodoxy in the "Diaspora"

As mentioned above, the fifth-century Canon 28 of Chalcedon refers to the territories outside the Greek-speaking world as "barbarian lands." That wording reflects a time when the ecclesiastical scene, in some ways at least, was considerably simpler than it is today. Yet, although this canon was never accepted by Rome, it has remained relevant to the East. It accords Constantinople a "primacy of honor" (a term that evidently allows a wide latitude of interpretation), and jurisdiction over churches outside the estab-lished episcopal sees of that era. This same canon is invoked by Orthodox Christians today on all sides of the primacy debate, and the question of how

17. See Norman P. Tanner, S.J., ed., *Decrees of the Ecumenical Councils,* vol. 2 (Washing-ton, DC: Georgetown University Press, 1990), 815-816, for the exact wording.

18. See his enthronement address in *In the World, Yet Not of the World,* 15-22, esp. 16-20.

to regulate the Orthodox who have found themselves in Western Europe and in the Americas, in Asia and Australia, has been a vexing one indeed. The Orthodox Christians, and their churches, finding themselves in these lands primarily through parallel immigrations stemming from Eastern Europe and the Middle East, have continued to coexist as parallel bodies with various kinds of ties to their mother churches, and these "parallel jurisdictions" are widely understood as constituting a canonical aberration. Once they leave their historic sees, do they all fall, as Constantinople contends, under Constantinople's jurisdiction? If so, how is that jurisdiction exercised? How do new local churches form? And how is autocephaly granted?

The last question has been one of the tests of the nature of Constantinopolitan primacy, particularly as focused in the odyssey of the Orthodox Church in America which, at Constantinople's original insistence, sought and received autocephaly from its mother church (the Moscow Patriarchate), and whose autocephaly remains unrecognized by Constantinople and a majority of the other local churches.

All this is mentioned by way of introduction to the complexity of the question of the "diaspora" churches,[19] setting the stage for what Patriarch Bartholomew has done, producing one of the first clear and potentially viable solutions to this problem. Less a solution than a mode of coexistence-in-transition, the Patriarch — through the mechanism of the Pan-Orthodox Pre-Conciliar meetings — has instituted "Episcopal Assemblies" that would coordinate the theological and pastoral activity of the churches along canonical norms, and aid in the articulation of a common witness to the church and to society.

The text of the decision that inaugurates these assemblies is worth exploring.[20] It is explicit about the provisional nature of the assemblies, seeing as a goal the ancient norm of "one bishop in each city." In this goal, it awaits the convening of "the future Great and Holy Council of the Orthodox Church," and is seen as part of the journey toward that council. The assemblies are to be chaired by the local hierarch representing the See of Constantinople, in view of the primatial status of that see. But significantly, the membership of the assemblies, and thus the Orthodox identity

19. The word *diaspora*, which I consistently place in quotation marks, is often contested in the Orthodox context because it seems to diminish the legitimacy of the local churches that have developed and thrived over the course of multiple centuries in the West, and enshrines their dependence upon mother churches in the historic sees.

20. See the Decision of the Fourth Pre-Conciliar Pan-Orthodox Conference, available online at http://www.scoba.us/resources/chambesy_documents/decision.html.

of the member churches, is determined by their communion with each other, and not with the See of Constantinople.[21]

These assemblies are only beginning their work at the time of this writing, making it difficult to assess their success. Despite their initial meetings, which have produced little other than increased mutual acquaintance, history may well reveal them to have been a creative and pastorally realistic move on the part of the Patriarch. Rather than solve or prejudge local canonical issues, they create appropriate mechanisms for their being addressed in a way that both acknowledges Constantinopolitan primacy and yet neither imposes nor forbids a maximal interpretation of it.

The Patriarch's attention to the churches outside the historic sees is an important part of a larger area of his ministry, which I will here mention only briefly despite its looming importance: the ministry of Orthodox unity. The "diaspora" issue, as we saw above, can find a more permanent solution only through a future "Great and Holy Council of the Orthodox Church." The promise of this event has been the object of considerable cynicism, with many observers believing that the Second Coming will easily outpace the arrival of the Great Council. And yet this movement towards a canonical regulation of the "diaspora" has logically emerged from the pre-conciliar process, meaning that the Council has, in a manner of speaking, already begun. The Patriarch has overseen that journey as part of his continuing work in serving the unity and coherence of the Orthodox Church, seen also in the meetings of heads of autocephalous Orthodox churches that he has regularly convened from early on in his tenure, for the first time in decades. The Patriarch's commitment to Orthodox unity, clarity, and coherence has resulted also in some disciplinary actions that have met with controversy, such as his censure of Athonite monasteries that refused to commemorate him as their charter requires. But this dimension of Constantinopolitan primacy — the ministry of the Church's unity and coherence — is universally agreed, and his faithful and consistent exercise of it has indelibly marked Patriarch Bartholomew's leadership.

Orthodoxy: Greek and Universal

Patriarch Bartholomew has striven to maintain the universal character of the Ecumenical Patriarchate, a character that transcends ethnic particular-

---

21. See above, in the context of the Ravenna Statement.

ities. Particularly as "ecumenical" means "universal," this would appear to be a redundancy and a non-issue; however, the maintenance of an identity that truly transcends Greekness has proved a considerable challenge on many levels. Owing to historical factors, the Orthodox Church has for centuries been called "Greek Orthodox." Although this is in fact a misleading translation of its identity as "Rum" or "Roman" Orthodox, it has been understood partly along linguistic lines — acknowledging the predominance of Greek in the Hellenized Near East as the language of the Scriptures and the early patristic and liturgical texts — as well as (far less justifiably so) along ethnic lines. This latter interpretation of Orthodoxy is a late development that can only be traced from the rise of nation-states and nationalism. But it has proved a difficult interpretation to leave behind.

It is against this backdrop that the Patriarch has sought actively to ensure that Greek Orthodoxy, and the Ecumenical Patriarchate specifically, be understood in universal and supra-ethnic terms, even while acknowledging the Hellenic character of many of the elements that have defined and spoken for the Church in history. The universality of the Patriarchate is something that would naturally be emphasized in the inter-Christian and interfaith spheres as well as in relation to society, particularly in so far as the Patriarch and Patriarchate are seen as essentially synonymous with Orthodoxy in the public eye. If the Patriarch is to be understood as the "spiritual head" of the Orthodox Church, as he is commonly called in the secular media, he must be seen not as a Greek leader of a Greek church, but as Ecumenical (i.e., universal) Patriarch. And he must be seen as such within the Orthodox Church as well.

Particularly with the continued rise of Orthodoxy in the West, and with the steady increase in the number of converts to Orthodoxy from other faiths, the Greekness of the Ecumenical Patriarchate has become an increasing point of tension. Patriarch Bartholomew has taken initiatives to emphasize the multi-ethnic character of his see: in particular he has expanded the Holy Synod of the Patriarchate to include hierarchs from dioceses outside of the Greek-speaking world. He has stressed that the Patriarchate of Constantinople today includes Albanians, Ukrainians, Carpatho-Russians, and Palestinians, with no attempt to Hellenize them in any way.[22]

---

22. This was stressed through a paper delivered at St. Vladimir's Orthodox Theological Seminary by Archimandrite (now Metropolitan) Elpidophoros Lambriniadis, later published as "Greek Orthodoxy, the Ecumenical Patriarchate, and Church in the USA," *St. Vladimir's Theological Quarterly* 54 (2010): 3-4.

While the Patriarch's insistence on the supra-ethnic character of the Patriarchate is critically important and canonically significant, it runs counter to common perceptions that owe to an array of contemporary factors: the Sacred and Holy Synod of the Patriarchate of Constantinople consists entirely of persons of Greek descent, whether they be of Turkish, Greek, Cypriot, or American nationality. Furthermore, while the Ecumenical Patriarchate encompasses Albanians, Ukrainians, and Carpatho-Russians, all of these came to the Patriarchate for refuge from local grievances or ecclesiastical complexities; thus their presence under the Ecumenical omophorion does not constitute a sign of its ecumenicity as such. And finally, the face of the Patriarchate in North and South America, the Greek Orthodox Archdiocese, is of a predominantly ethnic Greek character, in its hierarchy, clergy, composition, and liturgical, architectural, and musical style; its main seminary, the Holy Cross Greek Orthodox School of Theology, trains its students in Modern Greek, and the Greek national anthem is sung at their commencement exercises.

Each of these instances owes to historic and/or pastoral reasons, often out of the control of the current Patriarch, yet the cumulative effect on the perception within and outside the Orthodox world is powerful; they conspire to portray in most people's minds an undeniably ethnic-Greek character in the Ecumenical Patriarchate. All of this means that the Patriarch is fighting an uphill battle in showing that the essential reality is otherwise.

Concluding Remarks

I began this essay in drawing attention to the intra-Orthodox significance of the Patriarch's extra-Orthodox witness. Recalling that interrelationship, I would close by noting that many things are said of the Patriarch in the context of his witness to the world outside the Orthodox Church; several words consistently arise when describing him: courageous, a man of action, a pastor, a man of prayer, a person of theological erudition, a polyglot, cosmopolitan, an eminently accessible leader. Every one of these characterizations holds true for his leadership of the Orthodox Church, as it is perceived by the Orthodox themselves. Orthodox Christians may understand primacy in ways that, within a certain range, diverge. Some may be frustrated with the slowness of movement on issues such as that of the "diaspora." Some may object strenuously to the boldness of his approach to other Christians and/or other faiths. But it would be difficult for an Orthodox Christian to question the essential qualities enumerated above that Patriarch Bartholomew has embodied. Through those qualities, by God's grace, the Patriarch has moved the Orthodox Church significantly forward in relation to the world and to its own people, even as he has remained faithful to the timeless tradition of the Church of the Apostles.

CHAPTER 3

Ecumenical Patriarch Bartholomew and His Vision of the Ecumenical Movement and the World Council of Churches

Günther Gassmann

Prelude: The Patriarch in Historical Perspective

The person, work, and significance of His All Holiness Bartholomew I, Archbishop of Constantinople New Rome and Ecumenical Patriarch must be seen and described in a wide historical framework. Such a framework must encompass both the vertical dimension of the centuries-long history and presence of the Ecumenical Patriarchate, and the horizontal dimension of the worldwide coordinating responsibility of the Ecumenical Patriarchate for the communion of its member churches and the other autocephalous Orthodox churches of the world. This historical framework increasingly includes relations with other Christian communions, other living faiths, and not least concern for the social, moral, and ecological condition and future of humanity. This is the historical perspective in which Patriarch Bartholomew has to be seen and in which he sees himself. In this perspective we will consider the particular relation of the Patriarch to the ecumenical movement in general and the World Council of Churches (WCC) in particular.

While the Ecumenical Patriarchate of Constantinople began to play an important role in the emerging ecumenical movement in the twentieth century, it is possible to identify a few instances of pre-ecumenical contact. I mention only two that were connected with my own — Lutheran — confessional tradition. One of the important Lutheran confessional writings, the *Apology of the Augsburg Confession* of 1530, refers extensively to the "Greek Church," to the Orthodox theological and liturgical tradition, in order to indicate the broader Christian faith-tradition of which the Lutheran confession is a part.[1] The same Lutheran theologian and reformer who included in a positive, ecumenical spirit the references to the Greek Church — Philipp Melanchthon — arranged for a Greek translation of the central Lutheran Augsburg Confession. He sent it in 1559 to the Ecumenical Patriarch Jeremiah II of Constantinople. Fifteen years later another attempt to initiate a Lutheran-Orthodox dialogue was undertaken by prominent Lutheran theologians of Tübingen University. They again used the Greek translation of the Augsburg Confession. In the course of exchange of letters between 1543 and 1581 with Patriarch Jeremiah II — he sent three of them — different theological terminologies and thought-forms on both sides made mutual understanding impossible.[2] But it was a sign pointing to the future.

Three centuries after this prelude the Ecumenical Patriarchate entered the ecumenical scene with creative and extraordinary interchurch initiatives. In his Patriarchal and Synodical Encyclical of 1902 Patriarch Joachim III asked all local Orthodox churches in a still very reluctant and testing way whether "the present is judged to be the right time for a preliminary conference" in order to find points of encounter and contact with "the two great growths of Christianity, viz., the Western Church and the Church of the Protestants."[3] This extremely tentative approach was followed by a much more direct step in a foundational document of the ecumenical movement, the Encyclical of the Ecumenical Patriarchate of 1920, addressed "Unto the Churches of Christ Everywhere." Already its first sen-

---

1. For example, the *Apology* refers to the "Greek Church" as confirming the understanding of the real presence in the Eucharist (*Apology*, X, 2-3), as witnessing to the use of both kinds in the Lord's Supper (XXII, 4), as not practicing private Masses but only one public Mass and this only on Sundays (XXIV, 6), as not conceiving of the Mass a sacrifice for the living and dead (XXIV, 88, 93). See Robert Kolb and Timothy Wengert, eds., *The Book of Concord: The Confessions of the Evangelical Lutheran Church* (Minneapolis: Fortress Press, 2000), 184-185, 245-247, 258, 273-275.

2. Cf. George Mastranotonis, *Augsburg and Constantinople: The Correspondence between the Tübingen Theologians and Patriarch Jeremiah II of Constantinople on the Augsburg Confession* (Brookline: Holy Cross Orthodox Press, 2006); *Wort und Mysterium: Der Briefwechsel über Glauben und Kirche 1573 bis 1581 zwischen den Tübinger Theologen und dem Patriarchen von Konstantinopel*, ed. Evangelischen Kirche in Deutschland (EKD) (Witten: Luther-Verlag, 1958); Dorothea Wendebourg, *Reformation und Orthodoxie* (Göttingen: Vandenhoeck & Ruprecht, 1986).

3. Constantin G. Patelos, ed., *The Orthodox Church in the Ecumenical Movement: Documents and Statements, 1902-1975* (Geneva: WCC, 1978), 30-31 (27-33).

tence sets forth a daring vision: "Our own Church holds that rapprochement *(proseggisis)* between the various Christian Churches and fellowship *(koinonia)* between them is not excluded by the doctrinal differences which exist between them."[4] Here, the biblical concept of koinonia, which sixty years later became a key term in ecumenical statements, is introduced for the first time.[5] The newly founded League of Nations is paralleled with the idea of a "league between the churches" (the covering letter even more clearly relates the *"koinonia ton ethnon"* to the *"koinonia ton ekklesion"*). The encyclical proposes a number of forms of cooperation and new relationships.[6] The first General Secretary of the World Council of Churches after 1948, Willem A. Visser 't Hooft, wrote about its preparation:

> When the Holy Synod of the Church of Constantinople — the Ecumenical Patriarchate — met on 10 January 1919, it took an initiative which was without precedent in church history. It was officially decided to take steps to issue an invitation to all Christian churches to form a "league of churches." Thus the Church of Constantinople became the first church to plan for a permanent organ of fellowship and cooperation between the churches.[7]

An era of active ecumenical involvement of the Ecumenical Patriarchate and other Orthodox churches was inaugurated in a remarkable, pioneering way.

With the encyclical the door was opened for Orthodox participation that same year in the preparatory meetings of the Movements on Faith and Order and Life and Work, both being held in Geneva. A few years later this was followed by Orthodox participation in the World Conferences on Life and Work in 1925 at Stockholm and on Faith and Order in 1927 at Lausanne. In these and later conferences the wise, ecumenically outstanding representative of the Patriarchate, Patriarch Germanos of Thyatira (1872-1951), presented both his own papers and the series of separate declarations of the Orthodox delegates.[8] At the First Assembly of the World

---

4. *Ecumenical Review* 12 (October 1959): 79-82.

5. Patelos, *The Orthodox Church in the Ecumenical Movement*, 40, n. 1; W. A. Visser 't Hooft, *The Genesis and Formation of the World Council of Churches* (Geneva: World Council of Churches, 1982), 3-4.

6. Patelos, *The Orthodox Church in the Ecumenical Movement*, 41-42.

7. Visser 't Hooft, *The Genesis and Formation of the World Council of Churches*, 1 (cf. 1-8).

8. Patelos, *The Orthodox Church in the Ecumenical Movement*, 79-86, 137-131.

Council of Churches (WCC) in 1948 at Amsterdam the Patriarchate of Constantinople was, along with a few other Orthodox churches, among the founding members of the Council. Even today this remains a sign of the ecumenical commitment of the Patriarchate and Patriarchs.

Metropolitan Bartholomew Enters the Work of the WCC

In 1973, Bartholomew, a priest of the Ecumenical Patriarchate of Constantinople, was appointed Metropolitan of Philadelphia (Asia Minor). A few years later, after 1975, Metropolitan Bartholomew became a member of the WCC Commission on Faith and Order. This marked the beginning of his closer relationship with the WCC. From 1984 until 1991 — in 1990 he was elected Metropolitan of Chalcedon — Bartholomew served as vice-moderator of the Commission. During his time with Faith and Order Bartholomew was a member of the steering group for the study project Towards the Common Expression of the Apostolic Faith Today. We can well understand his interest in a study that was investigating the common tradition of the faith — especially in relation to the Nicene-Constantinopolitan Creed. At the WCC Assembly in Canberra in 1991 Bartholomew was elected a member of the WCC Central and Executive Committees before he was elected 270th Ecumenical Patriarch in 1991.

Between 1973 and 1991 the Ecumenical Patriarchate issued several important statements on the relationship between the Patriarchate and the WCC, most certainly with the help of the knowledgeable and ecumenically involved Bartholomew. The first of these was the Declaration of the Ecumenical Patriarchate on the Twenty-Fifth Anniversary of the WCC in 1973. The declaration lists positive achievements during the first twenty-five years of the WCC and mentions them by — implicitly — referring to Faith and Order studies in the 1960s and 1970s on Scripture and Tradition, patristics and councils, sacraments, and ordained ministry. All these "point to the positive presence of Orthodoxy in the Council," in which, furthermore, on the initiative of the Ecumenical Patriarchate, all Orthodox churches were now participating as members.[9] However, in a second step the declaration also points to the problem that has in some form or another accompanied and troubled the history of the WCC until today, namely, whether the WCC mainly should be a forum for social-political

9. Patelos, *The Orthodox Church in the Ecumenical Movement*, 60-61.

involvement or, on the other hand, a forum for theological discussions on divisive doctrinal differences between churches which are seeking ways towards unity. Referring to the Patriarchate as a faithful guardian of the doctrinal position of Orthodoxy, the declaration pleads for a proper balance between the different views on the mandate and exercise of the WCC.[10]

In a third step, the declaration lists eight concerns regarding the WCC. It emphasizes the role of the WCC as an organ and instrument of the churches (obviously against an independent authority of the Council) and indicates openness to possible membership of the Roman Catholic Church in the WCC while rejecting the inclusion into the WCC of movements and non-church groups — again, a consistently controversial topic in the history of the WCC. A balance between the necessity for profound theological study in the WCC (certainly the priority on the list) and of its engagement in projects of love and solidarity in addressing the manifold sufferings of human beings is again affirmed.[11] The response of the officers of the WCC Executive Committee in 1974 indicates openness on the part of the WCC to the concerns of the Patriarchate and for mutual understanding.[12]

The fortieth anniversary of the WCC in 1988 was for the history-conscious Ecumenical Patriarch the occasion for another message. This document relates the anniversary to the encyclical of 1920 and considers the foundation of the WCC a "fulfillment of its [i.e., the encyclical's] vision and realization of its proposal to form a 'League of Churches.'" It affirms that the presence in the WCC of the Ecumenical Patriarchate and of the whole Orthodox Church should be considered "natural" because of the universal character of the Orthodox Church. Indeed, this presence should be seen as "indispensable," because without Orthodox participation the WCC would represent only a fraction of Western Christendom; further, it should be regarded as "useful," because the presence of the Orthodox Church enriches the Council's theological thinking.[13]

The message also describes many of the WCC's positive achievements in theology, mission, diakonia, and Christian witness as the result and fruit of the Orthodox presence in the WCC. This presence, however, should become more substantial and representative both qualitatively and quantita-

10. Patelos, *The Orthodox Church in the Ecumenical Movement*, 62-63.
11. Patelos, *The Orthodox Church in the Ecumenical Movement*, 63-65.
12. Patelos, *The Orthodox Church in the Ecumenical Movement*, 66-68.
13. Gennadios Limouris, *Orthodox Visions of Ecumenism: Statements, Messages, and Reports on the Ecumenical Movement, 1902-1922* (Geneva: WCC Publications, 1994), 131.

tively — again, a longstanding Orthodox desideratum. Considering the future of the WCC, the Patriarchate looks forward with particular attention and expectation to the Commission on Faith and Order's study project Towards the Common Expression (Confession) of the Apostolic Faith Today. The enumeration of contemporary needs for the social activity of the WCC stresses the protection of the environment, "the good stewardship of which has been placed by God in our hands." The message ends with the assurance that the Patriarchate will continue its consistent and responsible cooperation with the WCC.[14]

In both these texts we find a number of the same elements:

- a strong awareness of the calling of the Patriarchate to be "spokesperson" for the Orthodox churches in relation to the ecumenical movement and the world;
- an expressive self-consciousness of the Patriarchate of the ecumenical-theological contribution of the Orthodox Church to the work and thinking of the WCC;
- a singular highlighting of the Faith and Order project of explicating the apostolic faith on the basis of the Nicene Creed; and
- a new emphasis on the preservation of the natural environment.

These last two points obviously correspond to the special concerns of Metropolitan Bartholomew, and their emphases and formulations are most probably due to his contribution.

Bartholomew's voice, concerns, and theological-ecumenical orientations became even more clearly recognizable after he was elected Ecumenical Patriarch in 1991. Jumping another twenty years from the fortieth anniversary of the WCC in 1988 to the sixtieth in 2008, we can hear his voice from a symbolically significant location, as he gave a homily in the city of the WCC (and John Calvin), Geneva, and from a Reformed pulpit, the Cathedral of St. Pierre in Geneva. This homily[15] presents a series of fundamental convictions, motivated by the anniversary, that are all especially important for this review of the Patriarch's relation to the ecumenical movement and the World Council of Churches.

---

14. Limouris, *Orthodox Visions of Ecumenism*, 132.

15. Homily by the Ecumenical Patriarch His All Holiness Bartholomew at the Sixtieth Anniversary of the World Council of Churches (2008). Available online at www.oikoumene .org/en/resources/documents/central-committee. Hereafter Homily.

The Emphatic Historical Orientation
of the Patriarchate and the Patriarch

The statements of the Patriarchate that we have already encountered contain a conscious and strong historical perspective. The reason for this orientation is twofold. First, for Orthodox self-understanding the history of the Holy Tradition of faith, sacramental life, and ministerial orders as revealed in Holy Scripture and affirmed by the seven Ecumenical Councils of the first centuries is normative for thinking about the present as well as the future. Second, this historical orientation and consciousness is inspired by the unique history of the Ecumenical Patriarchate, rooted in Canon 3 of the Council of Constantinople of 381 that states, "The Bishop of Constantinople shall have the prerogatives of honor after the Bishop of Rome, because Constantinople is New Rome."[16] In his homily in St. Pierre in Geneva in 2008 Bartholomew followed his predecessors in showing this historical sensitivity, referring to the beginning of the twentieth century when the churches began "establishing bonds of fellowship between divided churches and by building bridges to overcome their divisions." Like his predecessors, he again reminded his audience of the encyclical of 1920 and mentioned once again in understandable but modest pride the enthusiastic praise of the encyclical that, according to Visser 't Hooft, "sounded the clarion call to bring us together."[17]

However — and this is a sign of his broader ecumenical awareness — Bartholomew rests not with the acclaim of the encyclical but immediately sets it for the first time into a broader ecumenical context: "Far be it from me," he says, to suggest that "my church alone fathered the World Council of Churches."[18] Rather, he notes similar initiatives during the 1920s by American Anglican Bishop Charles Brent, a pioneer of the Faith and Order Movement (and president of the First World Conference in Faith and Order in 1927 at Lausanne), and Swedish Lutheran Archbishop Nathan Söderblom, a pioneer of the Life and Work Movement (and president of the First World Conference in 1925 at Stockholm) and a leader of the ecumenical movement in general. Preparatory conferences of both World Conferences were held at Geneva in 1920, the same year as the encyclical.

16. Cf. Timothy Ware, *The Orthodox Church* (Harmondsworth: Penguin, 1963), 31.

17. Homily, 1. Cf. also the statement by Visser 't Hooft in *The Genesis and Formation of the World Council of Churches*, 3-4.

18. In the original French version: "revendiquer la paternité du Consoeil Œcuménique."

Bartholomew concludes: "It can thus be stated that the concerted action by Orthodox, Anglican, and Reformation churches in the 1920s laid the foundations for the modern ecumenical movement and were among the originators of the formation of the World Council of Churches thirty years later."[19]

From the point of reference of its sixtieth anniversary, Bartholomew looks back at the foundation of the WCC at Amsterdam in 1948. Two years later came the necessary clarification of the nature of the new Council, formulated in the so-called Toronto Statement of 1950, which removed (especially Orthodox) fears of the WCC becoming a substitute for the churches (a "super-church") and trying to compel the churches to adopt positions contrary to their ecclesiological self-understanding. Only after this assurance had been given, believes the Patriarch, were the member churches free and able to determine the course of the WCC for their future work of implementing the tasks announced at its foundation. Finally, after mentioning a fruitful and positive period of thirty years of valuable work in the areas of theological study, mission and evangelism, Christian education, and many social justice issues, including human rights, poverty, and racial discrimination, the Patriarch refers to the "painful crisis" of the WCC in the years before the Eighth Assembly at Harare in 1998. It was a crisis, the Patriarch says, between those affirming different theological and ecclesiological traditions and representing diverse and distinctive interpretations of Holy Scripture as well as different (and divisive, I may add) perceptions of moral, social, and political issues. The response of the WCC to this crisis was the appointment and work of the Special Commission on Orthodox Participation in the WCC from 1998 through 2002, followed by the preparation of a new stage in the life of the Council. This episode in the history of the WCC was, according to the Patriarch, in the end a "healthy crisis," which led to a sincere dialogue that helped to overcome chronic difficulties that had poisoned relationships. This gave "a new impetus to continue our common journey along the path to unity."[20]

Behind this historical orientation lies Bartholomew's conviction, expressed in his address to the Plenary of Faith and Order in 2009, that openness to the past as well as to the future is an essential element of tradition. Tradition in the sense of comprehending the mind and spirit of the early church is neither "a sentimental attachment to the past nor an intellectual

19. Homily, 2.
20. Homily, 2-3.

fascination with Patristic literature." Neither does an orientation to the future imply a sense of escapism or otherworldliness. Rather, such an orientation offers a way out of the impasse of provincialism and confessionalism and enables us to believe that God's light is stronger than any darkness in the world.[21] This interconnectedness and integration of past and future is clearly expressed in its spiritual cohesion when the Patriarch, in a lecture in London's Westminster Abbey in 1995, says that the adherence to the one, undivided Church of the Apostles, the Fathers, and the Ecumenical Councils "shows the way not to the past, but to the future!"[22] Thus historical emphasis and Tradition serve as a key to understanding! This recalls the similar saying by the great Lutheran and later Orthodox historian of Christian doctrine, Jaroslav Pelikan (1923-2006), that "Tradition is the living faith of the dead, traditionalism is the dead faith of the living."[23]

The Patriarch and the Nature and Calling of the World Council of Churches

In Bartholomew's Geneva homily of 2008 the historical panorama again provides a framework for restating the nature and calling of the WCC. He describes the WCC as an interchurch platform that from its founding in 1948 has been at the service of its member churches in their efforts to seek Christian unity and facilitate cooperation in their social and diaconal work of addressing humanity's acute and urgent problems. He affirms that in the course of its sixty years of life the WCC has provided an "ideal platform where churches with different outlooks and belonging to a great variety of theological and ecclesiological traditions have been able to engage in dialogue and promote Christian unity, while all the time responding to the manifold needs of contemporary society."[24]

21. "Unity as Calling, Conversion, and Mission," Opening Address by His All Holiness the Ecumenical Patriarch Bartholomew to the Plenary of the World Council of Churches' Commission on Faith and Order (Crete: October 2009), 2. Available online at www.patriarchate .org/documents.

22. Lecture Given in Westminster Abbey on Visible Unity and Ecumenism for the Next Christian Millennium: Orthodox Perspective, 4 December 1995, 5. Available online at www .patriarchate.org/documents/next-christian-millennium.

23. See Jaroslav Pelikan, *The Vindication of Tradition* (New Haven: Yale University Press, 1984), 65.

24. Homily, 2-3.

Bartholomew then moves resolutely from this review and evaluation of the past to the future, considering the sixtieth anniversary as a "unique opportunity to turn together to the future and give new impetus, a new vision and renewed mandate to this fellowship ('communauté fraternelle'), which is what our sixty-year-old Council is."[25] This "fellowship" is characterized by the Patriarch — using a beloved formula in WCC circles — as "indisputably the most representative institutional expression of the ecumenical movement, now on its way to its centenary."[26] This formulation implies that the ecumenical movement is broader and more comprehensive than the WCC, since Roman Catholic ecumenism, the bilateral dialogues of Christian World Communions, and ecumenical initiatives outside the WCC are also constituent elements of the ecumenical movement. When considering Bartholomew's words that the WCC is "on its way to its centenary," it came to my mind that only a Christian leader with such a wide historical horizon could have made such a fascinating, far-flung statement, looking toward the year 2048 as if it were around the corner.

Bartholomew then describes how in the years of important work between about 1950 and 1980 two very distinct trends became apparent in the life of the WCC; I believe these two trends or tendencies mark the orientation and work of the WCC today. One trend could be characterized, according to Bartholomew, as the ecclesiastical one; it considers the ecumenical task to be reaching doctrinal and organizational unity between the churches by emphasizing and discussing the content of faith, church order, and structures. The other tendency is more pragmatic, considering ecumenism mainly as action by the churches in the world and for the world and seeking "to make the faithful aware of Christ's presence in all social, scientific, and political activity." In the "endless animated discussions" about these two orientations of the nature and mission of the WCC there are also, according to the Patriarch, other voices, particularly from Orthodox churches, that criticize these one-sided concepts. For them — and obviously for Bartholomew — true ecumenism should strive both for Christian unity and be equally concerned about the evils afflicting today's world. This leads him to the following conclusion:

> In fact, in the course of the sixty years of its life, the Council has provided an ideal platform where churches, with different outlooks and belonging

25. Homily, 1.
26. Homily, 2.

to a great variety of theological and ecclesiological traditions, have been able to engage in dialogue and promote Christian unity, while all the time responding to the manifold needs of contemporary society.[27]

It is remarkable how Bartholomew pleads for a balance between both these stances. Theologians from Orthodox, Reformation (especially Lutheran), and also theologically minded Evangelical churches have often criticized what they have regarded as a one-sided social activist emphasis of much of the work of the WCC in terms of programs, finances, personnel, and general outlook. The Patriarch certainly knows this, but he obviously sees a response to this continuing issue in the life of the WCC in the conscious and determined holding together of the two emphases, seeing them in a balance and interrelation of equal importance. As he remarks in the Geneva homily, "I am glad of the fact that the Council still has at the center of its work the vision of its member churches to achieve, by God's grace, their unity." Accordingly, the paramount importance and role of the WCC, and especially of its Faith and Order division, consist in the difficult and essential task of careful and inclusive study of the "ecclesiological issues that affect the very being of the Council and the quest for Christian unity." This emphatic affirmation, in fact, underlines the statement in the Constitution of the WCC that the "primary purpose of the fellowship of churches in the WCC is to call one another to visible unity in one faith and one Eucharistic fellowship, expressed in worship and common life in Christ."[28] And Bartholomew adds in a kind of "parallelism of members" (to borrow a term from the study of literature and the Psalms) a similar formulation:

> I am so happy that the Ninth Assembly has confirmed the calling of the World Council of Churches in regard to the Church's presence in society by recognizing its role as catalyst in establishing peace in the world, promoting interfaith dialogue, defending human dignity, combating violence, protecting the environment, and being in solidarity with those in need.[29]

This is to incarnate God's truth and love as fully as possible in view of the final judgment on whether Christians have lived in the Spirit of Christ. It is

---

27. Homily, 2-3.

28. Constitution and Rules. Available online at www.oikoumene.org/en/resources/documents/assembly/porto-alegre-2006.

29. Homily, 3.

significant how, for Bartholomew, the eschatological future is here and now anticipated and becomes determinative and judgmental on the present reality of Christian and ecclesial life.

As a kind of reaffirmation of this last statement, the Patriarch adds at the end of his homily, like a kind of postscript, the exhortation to acknowledge that the differences in the responses of churches to moral problems are not necessarily insurmountable and that dialogue on ethical and moral questions should be conducted with the assumption that the churches are not content to agree to disagree on their respective moral teachings "but that they are prepared to confront their divergences honestly, and examine them in the light of doctrine, worship life, and Holy Scripture."[30] Even though the Patriarch does not here take a particular position on any of the social-ethical problems discussed in the WCC, his words are a strong and courageous affirmation of the commitment to dialogue and struggle about the truth. He speaks in the midst of a particular, new, sensitive context, aware of the dangers of division between churches over differences on ethical issues which may be even more difficult to cope with than the classical doctrinal differences. The Patriarch calls the churches not to passively accept their differences or simply find a way to live with them; rather, he pleads in favor of facing and struggling with these issues in an open way. He is more free to do so, I believe, because the restatement of the relations between the Orthodox churches and the WCC on the basis of the recommendations of the Special Commission on Orthodox Participation in the WCC makes sure that no church or group of churches can impose its position on other member churches of the WCC by means of majority decisions.

In his homily the Patriarch also weighs in on current discussions about a "reconfiguration" of the ecumenical movement. The WCC, he says, should not gradually be reduced to the mere role of "animator," by sharing out its responsibilities to other organizations, taking away its major ecumenical role, or setting up new ecumenical instruments to "perform tasks that properly belong to the raison d'être of the Council." The WCC should remain at the center of the life of the global ecumenical village. It is impressive how the Patriarch appears here as a staunch defender of the original status and role of the WCC. Consequently, he challenges WCC member churches to reaffirm the role of the Council as a privileged ecumenical space where the churches are free to create networks for social services and uphold the important values they share, and where the churches through

---

30. Homily, 5.

dialogue will continue to break down barriers that separate them. He calls the churches to renew their confidence in "this Council of ours as a useful and necessary instrument as we attempt to respond to social and ethical questions" because the member churches belong to one fellowship by confessing together the Lord Jesus Christ as God and Savior.[31]

At a time when the World Council of Churches has lost quite a bit of its former standing and public presence among the churches — not only because of financial difficulties and staff reductions and the emergence of other strong nongovernmental organizations, but also because of its lack of a clear profile and convincing priorities in the years before 2010 — it is highly impressive and encouraging that at such a difficult time the Ecumenical Patriarch courageously and forcefully calls the churches back to confidence in and support of their Ecumenical Council. His commitment is reciprocated by the World Council's support of and solidarity with the Ecumenical Patriarchate, manifested by the many visits of officers and staff members of the WCC to Phanar and to the Theological School of Halki, which is waiting for permission from the Turkish government to be reopened for its original purpose of theological studies and Christian education. It could well be that Halki will become a central institution for Orthodox studies, not only for the worldwide Orthodox community but also for students and researchers from other churches.

One remarkable visit from the WCC to Phanar took place from 13 to 16 December 2006. At this meeting the Patriarch underlined in his opening words the Patriarchate's long association with the WCC and its profound commitment to the WCC as expressed, for instance, by the strong presence of the Patriarchate on commissions of the WCC. In their response, the officers of the WCC praised the Patriarch as a leading figure in the ecumenical movement.[32] Not coincidentally, such visits have also led visitors to request their respective governments to plead with the Turkish government in favor of more religious liberty for the Patriarchate and of allowing the Theological School at Halki to resume its activities.

Another example of the support of the Patriarchate and Patriarch by the WCC can be seen in the official letters of the general secretary of the WCC in 2004 and 2006 (the former together with the general secretary of the Conference of European Churches). These documents express solidar-

31. Homily, 4.
32. Meeting of the World Council of Churches Officers, Phanar, 13-16 December 2006. Available online at www.ec-patr.org.

ity and support by the European churches and the worldwide fellowship of the WCC for the Ecumenical Patriarchate in its precarious situation of being exposed to hostilities and isolation. They confront government attempts to challenge the word *Ecumenical* in the Patriarch's title by highlighting the extraordinary ecumenical significance of the Patriarchate since the attribution of that title in the sixth century (and later followed by contacts with Lutheran theologians in the sixteenth century; see above) up to the present time. For today the Patriarch is actively involved in facilitating and coordinating dialogues with other churches as well as supporting interreligious dialogue, working at reconciliation and peace among different peoples and cultures, exercising a leading role in important initiatives for the protection of the environment, and, not least, unfailingly supporting the WCC.[33]

The Patriarch and the Ecumenical Goal of Christian Unity

The present Ecumenical Patriarch is an especially forceful and outspoken advocate of the churches' ongoing search for Christian unity and of the place and mandate of the World Council of Churches as the representative instrument for serving the dreams and efforts of the churches in the ecumenical movement. How does the Patriarch delineate the goal of that movement's pilgrimage towards visible unity? For most Orthodox voices in the past the answer was clear: the Orthodox Church "believes itself to be the 'one, holy, catholic, and apostolic Church,' of which the Creed speaks." This implies that the divisions within Christianity do not directly involve the Orthodox Church and the overcoming of divisions would involve — respecting a certain measure of diversity and excluding any form of submission under Orthodoxy — the reunion and reconciliation with the Orthodox Church.[34] How is this traditional position reinterpreted by the present Ecumenical Patriarch?

In his 1995 lecture in Westminster Abbey in London the Ecumenical Patriarch introduced his view in a twofold perspective. First, the concern

33. Letter from the WCC and the Conference of European Churches to His All Holiness Ecumenical Patriarch Bartholomew, 10 December 2004. Available online at www.patriarchate.org/documents/www-and-cec-2004. Letter to His All Holiness Bartholomew, Ecumenical Patriarch of Constantinople, 29 August 2007. Available online at www.oikoumene.org/resources/documents/general-secretary.

34. Cf. Ware, *The Orthodox Church*, 315-319.

for visible unity is historically a major task of the ecumenical movement and especially of the WCC, together with Vatican II, the theological dialogues, and other ecumenical endeavors. Second, the concern for visible unity is conceived in a theological, biblical, spiritual perspective as the great gift of unity as Jesus Christ wished it (see John 17:21-22) and the Holy Spirit gives it, and this to the glory of God the Father. In a wonderful way the Patriarch contextualizes and grounds Christian unity in a Trinitarian and doxological framework. However, and here enters the outspoken realism of Bartholomew, visible unity as the main goal of the ecumenical movement is overshadowed by the visible disunion of Christians. Sadly, we Christians are entering the Third Millennium as children of disgrace instead of unity.[35]

One response to this realistic view on the ecumenical (and even intra-Orthodox) situation is, according to the Patriarch, to stress and establish even more actively the visible unity of the Orthodox churches because "when the unity of one of the Christian families is strengthened, the unity of the whole body is strengthened." Accordingly, despite failures and disappointments, the pursuit of the restoration of unity and of — again Bartholomew's broader vision — the unity of the whole humanity is an urgent task and belongs to the sacred obligation of Orthodoxy to participate actively in the ecumenical movement.[36] The absolute commitment of the Patriarch to the ecumenical cause and his critique, often bitter and angry, of Christian divisions and even intra-Orthodox anti-ecumenical voices[37] are a mark of his sober and steadfast stance. At the same time he stretches his vision on unity to its outer limits by including all people.

Twelve years later, in 2007, the Patriarch presented a meditation at the opening prayer service of the Third European Ecumenical Assembly at Sibiu in Romania. These European Ecumenical Assemblies are jointly organized by the Conference of European Churches (CEC) and the Council of European Bishops' Conferences (CCEE). In Sibiu in 2007 Bartholomew once again chose a historical approach, moving through the preceding two European Assemblies — Basel 1989 and Graz 1997 — back to the Patriarchate's invitation to other churches over a hundred years ago "to cooperate for the full restoration of Christian communion and unity, as well as for

---

35. Lecture Given in Westminster Abbey on Visible Unity and Ecumenism, 3.

36. Lecture Given in Westminster Abbey on Visible Unity and Ecumenism, 5.

37. Patriarchal Encyclical on the Sunday of Orthodoxy 2010. Available online at www .patriarchate.org/documents/sunday-orthodoxy-2010.

the support of suffering humanity."[38] Having this historical background established, the Patriarch emphatically affirms:

> We repeat and emphasize that all of Orthodoxy, and our modesty personally, remain unwavering and unmoved in our conviction that we are obliged to do everything in our power to promote the sacred work of restoration of full ecclesiastical and sacramental communion among Christians on the basis of the same faith in love and respect for the particular expressions within which the apostolic faith is expressed.[39]

It is impressive how the Patriarch adds here to the familiar formula "full ecclesiastical and sacramental communion" the qualification "in respect for the particular expressions within which the apostolic faith is expressed." With this short addition any idea of unity in the sense of uniformity is excluded, and even though the nature and degree of diversity must remain rather general in such a short remark it nevertheless opens possible spaces for the recognition of Christian diversity within agreed boundaries of unity.

Such diversity within unity is, in fact, also alluded to when the Patriarch draws on the key biblical text on Christian unity, John 17:20-21, and interprets the phrase "that they all may be one *as* [emphasis mine] you, Father, are in me and I am in you." He interprets this saying as indicating a model for the restoration of Christian unity that corresponds to the life and manner of existence among the three divine persons of the Triune God. The impetus of this prayer of Christ obliges Christians to seek to realize full communion among the churches "instead of the individual interests for the increase of our own power and influence, or else the overemphasis of exclusion and ecclesiastical uniqueness." In order to move towards such communion the Patriarch strongly underlines that it is absolutely necessary to promote and support theological dialogue because without dialogue it is impossible to achieve the ultimate goal of Christian reconciliation, communion, and unity.[40] The Patriarch envisions a form of Christian unity that is not based on sterile uniformity but embraces a measure of diversity of faith-expressions that are not contradictory but, like the model of the three di-

---

38. Meditation of His All Holiness the Ecumenical Patriarch Bartholomew in the Opening Prayer Service of the Third European Ecumenical Assembly in Sibiu 2007. Available online at www.patriarchate.org/documents/. Hereafter Meditation.

39. Meditation, 3.

40. Meditation, 3.

vine persons, are related in their diversity to their essential common ground and being: the divine gift of unity and communion.

Perhaps the most illustrative text for Bartholomew's ecumenical convictions is his homily in St. Pierre in Geneva on 17 February 2008. Its biblical text leads directly into the crucial issue of division and unity: St. Paul's challenge to the Christians of Corinth, torn by quarrels, that there should be no divisions among them but they should be united in the same mind and the same purpose (1 Cor. 1:10). Bartholomew interprets St. Paul's rebuke of the Corinthians as a reminder "that division in the Church contradicted its nature, damaged its witness, and caused its mission in the world to fail."[41] He relates this general and sharp conclusion directly to the celebration of the sixtieth anniversary of the WCC.

It was this truth of the gospel, he says, that inspired the mobilization of our churches at the beginning of the twentieth century. When they were confronted with the "scandal of division," they directed their attention to the urgent question of Christian unity and began to establish "bonds of fellowship between divided churches" and to "build bridges to overcome their divisions." One of these bridges became the WCC.[42] It is interesting and remarkable that the Patriarch speaks of "our churches" in a way that includes the Orthodox Church, and that he dares to refer to the "scandal of division."[43] However, his emphasis lies on the response to this scandal. He speaks in warm and positive words about the work of the WCC to help the churches overcome their divisions and move in theological dialogue, social cooperation, and mutual love toward their vision "to achieve, by God's grace, their unity in the one faith and around the same Eucharistic table."[44]

This short formulation of the goal is further illuminated when Bartholomew defines the dialogue between the churches as the way to break down the barriers preventing them from "recognizing one another as churches confessing a common faith, administering the same baptism, and celebrating the Eucharist together, so that the community, which is what they now are, can become a *communion* [emphasis mine] in the faith, in sacramental life and in witness."[45] In the words of the Patriarch we find elements that are often enumerated as being fundamental and essential for

41. Homily, 1.

42. Homily, 1.

43. In the earlier stages of the ecumenical movement there were long discussions regarding whether one could call the divisions between the churches "sinful" or "a scandal."

44. Homily, 3.

45. Homily, 4.

the unity of the churches. This open way in which Bartholomew indicates basic elements of unity — though certainly not all such elements — provides a space in which dialogue can develop without stumbling immediately over a too high barrier of conditions. Meanwhile, other more difficult questions, such as Orthodox views on Tradition, Church, and apostolic ministry, can be discussed after some first common steps have been achieved. This is, therefore, an open, unconditional invitation to dialogue. This dialogue, conducted with good results already on the world level, in Europe, the United States, and Australia, does not start from zero but is based on an already existing fellowship between the churches, which has been rediscovered and made visible through the ecumenical movement and the encounters between the churches. I believe that it is this kind of fellowship to which the Patriarch frequently refers.

The existing fellowship is also implied when the Patriarch, in his Message to the Ninth Assembly of the WCC in Porto Alegre in 2006, mentions the Special Commission on Orthodox Participation in the WCC. There he says that "for the first time in the history of the WCC fundamental questions raised by the Orthodox churches were also shared by other member churches."[46] In this joint search for more satisfactory forms of Orthodox involvement in the work of the WCC Bartholomew obviously sees a test of the strength of the fellowship that has developed in the history of the WCC, a fellowship that also can face difficult issues without breaking. This fellowship is the basis, according to Bartholomew's homily in Geneva in 2006, for moving forward toward the goal of visible unity, the communion — koinonia — of the churches (see above). Bartholomew uses here the term *communion/koinonia* that has become central in recent reflections on Christian unity. It was, for instance, the leading perspective of the discussions at the Fifth World Conference on Faith and Order at Santiago de Compostela in 1993,[47] in the preparations for which Bartholomew was also involved.

It must have been a special joy for the Patriarch to come one year after his homily in Geneva to Crete in October 2009 to meet with "our beloved

46. Message from His All Holiness Ecumenical Patriarch Bartholomew I to the Ninth Assembly of the WCC, 2 February 2006. Available online at www.oikoumene.org/en/resources/documents/assembly/porto-alegre-2006.

47. Thomas F. Best and Günther Gassmann, eds., *On the way to Fuller Koinonia: Official Report of the Fifth World Conference on Faith and Order* (Geneva: WCC Publications, 1994), especially chapters 3 and 4, the Message of the World Conference, and the Report of Section I on the Understanding of Koinonia and Its Implications.

Faith and Order Commission" — beloved, I assume, because the Commission has been an important part of his ecumenical involvement from 1975 to 1991 and because this meeting took place twenty-five years after the meeting of the Faith and Order Standing Committee in the same place in 1984, when Metropolitan Bartholomew was appointed to the Steering Group of the Apostolic Faith Study. As the new director of Faith and Order, this was my first occasion to work together with him. In 2009 the Patriarch spoke on "Unity as Calling, Conversion, and Mission." In the first section, on "Unity as Calling," he approaches the unity theme in a rather uncommon manner by taking an apophatic perspective, saying that the call to unity lies beyond or before all human intellectual and theological reasoning. He pleads for considering the search for Christian unity in a spirit of forbearance and patience, of patient expectation that the persistent pursuit of unity will be fulfilled in God's time and granted by his heavenly grace.[48] He does not thereby advocate pious Christian passivity, but a calm, God-trusting attitude that can move beyond the frustrations caused by disagreements and divisions.

In his second section, on "Unity as Conversion," Bartholomew continues in this spiritual and pastoral vein, an unusual strategy given that many texts on Christian unity are filled with concepts and strategies. He pleads for conversion to a profound sense of humility in approaching efforts towards Christian unity. He calls for mutual learning instead of imposing one's own ways on others, which would be, in his straightforward way of putting it, "arrogant and hypocritical." Rather, he encourages us to learn from "the early Fathers and Mothers of the Church" (an unusual and daring formulation for an Orthodox Hierarch). This Tradition connects us with the past and the future.[49] The common calling and conversion of the churches should lead, according to the third section on "Unity in Mission," to a discernment of the common ministry and mission to which the churches are called. This ministry understands the patient and persistent pursuit of God's gift of unity, the advocacy and work for justice and peace in the world, and the commitment to the preservation of the land as God's creation and gift. In an attitude of meekness, the Patriarch emphasizes, Christians should turn humbly toward their common roots in the Apostolic Church and the Communion of Saints and to their common future in

---

48. "Unity as Calling, Conversion, and Mission," in Best and Gassmann, eds., *On the Way to Fuller Koinonia*, 1-2.

49. Best and Gassmann, eds., *On the Way to Fuller Koinonia*, 2.

the perspective of God's kingdom. In this spiritual dimension they are set free for an authentic and prophetic criticism of the world's consumerism and an attitude of caring and sharing for the benefit of of God's creation.[50] Once again we find in this text the consistent interrelation of major interests and concerns of the Patriarch which are held together in a broad spiritual vision that connects heaven and earth/land, past and future, church and world, faith and action — a truly "ecumenical" vision.

Postlude: A Truly Ecumenical Patriarch

His All Holiness Patriarch Bartholomew I, who occasionally likes to call himself "our Modesty," deserves the title "Ecumenical" not simply for historical and canonical reasons. He is also an "Ecumenical" Patriarch in the most direct and specific sense of being a servant of the whole church for the whole world. This becomes again apparent when one summarizes what has been put together on the preceding pages.

First, one impression that immediately becomes apparent is the way in which Patriarch Bartholomew consistently speaks, thinks, and writes out of a lively knowledge and consciousness of the history of the ecumenical movement and of the World Council of Churches (WCC) and the active involvement in it of the Ecumenical Patriarch. This brings to expression an understanding of Christian Tradition that interconnects past, present, and future in the horizon of the presence and guidance of God, the Holy Trinity.

Second, speaking thus out of a profound historical awareness leads Bartholomew to express his considerations and formulate his observations and ideas in a realistic manner, often stated in sober, down-to-earth sentences in which he rejoices about the WCC's positive achievements and clearly points to its weaknesses and crises.

Third, in his addresses, homilies, statements, and lectures the Patriarch comes out as an unshakable and firm advocate and supporter of the ecumenical movement and the WCC. His faithfulness and commitment to the calling and service of the WCC as a precious instrument of the churches are equaled only by a few other church leaders. This makes him a defender of the traditional structure, role, and mandate of the WCC (not excluding certain modifications).

Fourth, the Patriarch takes his stand between the different ecumenical

---

50. Best and Gassmann, eds., *On the Way to Fuller Koinonia*, 3.

concepts that have since 1948 often strained the relations between WCC member churches. He is consciously holding together the theological work of the WCC in preparing ways towards visible unity between the churches and the social-ethical engagement of the WCC in helping to alleviate the pressing needs of humanity. Both orientations and emphases of the WCC belong together, both are jointly serving God's gracious purpose.

Fifth, rooted in biblical and patristic insights, the Patriarch indicates the contours of Christian unity by stretching out from the already existing fellowship in the WCC towards a future communion/koinonia in apostolic faith and sacraments, affirmed in mutual recognition of churches, and by following the model of Trinitarian relationships allowing for a certain measure of diversity in expressions of faith.

Sixth, the Patriarch moves in his thoughts from a deeply spiritual and doxological approach toward an all-encompassing worldview or world-conception that interrelates and intermediates efforts for Christian unity, for reconciliation and peace in society and world, for dialogue and understanding with other monotheistic religions, and efforts for the care and preservation of the environment — "the created nature as the extended body of Christ."[51]

It was for me a special joy, inspiration, and privilege to often meet and work together with this extraordinary ecumenical personality and leader during my time directing the Secretariat of Faith and Order in Geneva.

---

51. Discerning God's Presence in the World, Fordham University, 2009, 3. www .patriarchate.org/documents/discerning-gods-presence-in-the-world.

CHAPTER 4

Faith at the Margins: Ecumenical Patriarch Bartholomew as Bridge Builder

Dale T. Irvin

> *If unity — as our own ongoing and persistent goal — is indeed a gift of God, then it demands a profound sense of humility and not any prideful insistence. This means that we are called to learn from others as well as to learn from time-tested formulations. It also implies that imposing our ways on others — whether "conservative" or "liberal" — is arrogant and hypocritical. Instead, genuine humility demands from all of us a sense of openness to the past and the future; in other words, much like the ancient god Janus, we are called to manifest respect for the time-tested ways of the past and regard for the heavenly city that we seek (cf. Heb. 13:14). This "turning" toward the past and the future is surely part and parcel of conversion.*

The above words were part of the address by His All Holiness Patriarch Bartholomew delivered at the Faith and Order Plenary Commission meeting in October 2009.[1] As the 270th successor to the head of the church founded by St. Andrew in Byzantium and the spiritual leader of Orthodox Christians throughout the world today, Bartholomew knows well what it means to "learn from time-tested formulations" and to treat "the time-

---

1. "Unity as Calling, Conversion, and Mission," Opening Address by His All Holiness the Ecumenical Patriarch Bartholomew to the Plenary of the World Council of Churches' Commission on Faith and Order, Crete, October 2009. Available online at http://www.patriarchate .org/documents/addresses-plenary-wcc.

tested ways of the past" with respect. Continuity with tradition infuses every word, every statement, and every act of the Patriarch. At the same time, he has proven to be one of the most innovative leaders to have occupied the patriarchal office in centuries. Bartholomew's leadership in the relatively new field of environmental theology has earned him the attribution of "Green Patriarch." His openness to ecumenical life and work, and especially his efforts to build bridges with other Christians and with peoples of other religions have made him one of the important voices of any faith tradition speaking for dialogue and peace in the world today. By all accounts he has demonstrated a profound willingness to learn from others who live beyond the boundaries of Orthodoxy or who represent forms of intellectual life and faith that are not usually associated with the Great Tradition of Orthodox Christianity.

The Patriarch's words appear to be even more poignant when seen against the backdrop of continuing political pressure and at times persecution that have been directed against him at home in Istanbul, and the continuing challenges faced by the Orthodox churches for which he seeks to provide leadership around the world. The humility of which the Patriarch often speaks is partly an expression of his profound spiritual commitment and partly a function of the historical realities in which he finds both himself personally and the office that he occupies. The Ecumenical Patriarch has lived under debilitating circumstances that have historically humbled the office for centuries. Phanar (meaning "lantern" or "lighthouse" in Greek), the district in Istanbul in which the patriarch has resided since 1599 and in which the patriarchal offices are located, is hardly comparable to the Vatican, its counterpart in Rome. Although Bartholomew sees himself as the spiritual leader of Orthodoxy throughout the world and as having direct jurisdiction of churches on four continents, the Patriarchate has nothing comparable to the administrative bureaucracy that runs the Vatican. One needs only to think on the one hand of the Pontifical Gregorian University, the Angelicum (the Pontifical University of St. Thomas Aquinas), the Pontifical Lateran University, the Pontifical University of the Holy Cross, the Pontifical Urbaniana University, and the Pontifical University Antonianum, all in Rome; and on the other of the now-closed Holy Theological School of Halki on an island off the coast of Istanbul in the Sea of Marmara to see the contrast.

The seminary at Halki is a fitting symbol of the struggle that the Patriarchate has faced in its recent history. Founded in 1844 by Patriarch Germanos IV at the top of the Hill of Hope on the island of Halki, the

Dale T. Irvin

school was initially intended to be a center for renewal in Orthodox learning and to confront the growing challenges (both religious and secular) coming from the West. Its graduates and professors served on various committees of the Holy and Sacred Synod of the Ecumenical Patriarchate and in other offices of leadership throughout the Orthodox world. Today the school sits closed, however. Accessible only by foot or carriage (there are no cars allowed on the island), its grounds continue to house an important library containing numerous ancient manuscripts and to provide the Patriarch with a place for spiritual refuge, but no classes are held and no new graduates are being produced. A provision in the 1961 Turkish Constitution that required all private schools to be under state supervision proved to be its undoing. The Turkish government closed the theological school in 1971 when its trustees refused to come under state supervision. Considerable international efforts reaching all the way to the highest levels of diplomacy in Western Europe and the United States have still not reversed the decision.

The place of Bartholomew's upbringing mirrors the difficulties of Halki and the patriarchate itself in Turkey. He was born on the island of Imbros in the Aegean Sea. Although the majority of its inhabitants were historically of Greek ethnicity, Imbros, or Gökçeada as the island is now known, was made part of Turkey in 1923 by the Treaty of Lausanne, which ended the Ottoman Empire and established the modern nation of Turkey. During the 1960s the Turkish government, fearing a Greek independence movement on the island, began a program of systematic discrimination, taking land for public purposes such as building prisons and forcing most of the island's 8,000 Greek inhabitants to emigrate. The island is now mostly Turkish in ethnicity. Only 300 or so Greeks remain. The town in which Bartholomew grew up, which was known then as Holy Theodores, is now the Village of Olive Trees.

Bartholomew completed his undergraduate studies at Halki in 1961 and then served two years of mandatory duty in the Turkish military before heading to Rome, where he studied in the Pontifical Oriental Institute in the Gregorian, to Bossey, Switzerland, where he studied in the Ecumenical Institute, and to Munich, where he studied at the University of Munich. He returned to Turkey in 1968 to serve as assistant dean at Halki, and in 1972 became the personal and administrative secretary to his predecessor, Patriarch Demetrios. Upon Demetrios' death, the Holy Synod presented eight names to the Turkish government for consideration and approval as candidates for the next patriarch. All were accepted, and Bartholomew was subsequently elected to the office.

64

The fact that the members of the Holy Synod had to wait to hear from the Turkish government concerning the acceptability of the candidates under consideration for patriarch points to the significant and enduring political challenges posed to the ancient office by virtue of it being located physically in Istanbul today. Bartholomew, like every patriarch since 1923, is a citizen of Turkey. The Turkish government recognizes him only as the spiritual leader of the small community of Greek Orthodox Christians in Turkey and not as the spiritual leader of Orthodox Christians in other parts of the world. The government officially refers to him as the Roman Orthodox Patriarch in Phanar, and not as the Ecumenical Patriarch. Turkish law requires the patriarch and other members of the Holy Synod to be citizens of the state. In 2004 Bartholomew began appointing bishops to the Holy Synod who did not have Turkish citizenship, challenging the requirement that members be only Turkish in national identity. In 2010 the Turkish government agreed to extend citizenship to a number of archbishops in the Greek Orthodox communion from around the world, thereby increasing the number of candidates who can be considered for the next patriarch and implicitly recognizing the wider ecumenical nature of the Patriarchate without abandoning the principle of Turkish national identity of the church.

Under Turkish law the Patriarchate has no legal standing as a religious corporation or body. Turkish law in fact does not recognize the legality of any religious corporation or body. Private foundations of a nonreligious nature are allowed to own property in Turkey, which they can administer on behalf of a religious body, but the religious corporation itself has no legal standing. After 1923 the new Turkish Republic established a Presidency of Religious Affairs, or the *Diyanet,* to take over many of the religious functions that had previously come under the office of the *Şeyhülislam* that had served as the religious body advising sultans of the Ottoman Empire. The *Diyanet,* whose offices are appointed and funded by the Turkish government, is charged with overseeing matters pertaining to worship, belief, and daily practice of Islam, the religion of the vast majority of people in Turkey. The *Diyanet* appoints all imams in mosques throughout Turkey, promotes ongoing scholarship, oversees officially required religious education in public schools, and provides legal opinions regarding the practice of Islam within Turkish society. Mosques and other properties are owned by municipal governments or private individuals. The local community of Muslims has no legal standing as a corporation in Turkey. Furthermore, the *Diyanet* has no say in matters pertaining to other religions practiced in Turkey. Those other religions remain virtually invisible to the state.

Such political invisibility is a far cry from the days when the bishop of Constantinople exercised considerable power within the Byzantine Empire. The conversion of the Roman imperial order in the fourth century of the Common Era had a far-reaching effect upon Christianity globally. The relocation of the capital of the Roman Empire to the city of Byzantium, which was renamed Constantinople, transformed the bishopric that had historically been related to the efforts of St. Andrew considerably. Constantinople became the Second Rome and its bishop was elevated accordingly in dignity and privileges within the empire. In the sixth century the bishop of Constantinople began to be known as the ecumenical patriarch. Given his proximity to the Roman emperor who resided in Constantinople, and the dignity with which his office was invested by other bishops in the Greek-speaking world, the ecumenical patriarch came to exercise a significant amount of judicial authority within the Eastern Roman Empire. Such authority, and even the use of the title "ecumenical patriarch," became a point of contention with his counterpart in the First Rome, the bishop of Rome, or the pope. Several times the two heads of imperial Christendom fell out of communion with one another, the most enduring being in the eleventh century when the two offices traded mutual excommunications that have still to be fully healed.

In the seventh century the Eastern Roman Empire, with its capital in Constantinople, began to lose territories to armies of Arabs who were guided by the faith called Islam. Where the Arabs asserted their political and administrative control, the official religion became Islam. Christians in these regions were already beginning to fracture into separate theological communions, driven mostly by debates surrounding the relationship of the divine and human nature or person in Jesus Christ that were the focus of the Council of Chalcedon in 451, but also fueled by political dissent and cultural differences within the Byzantine world. Significant numbers of Christians in Armenia, Syria, Palestine, Persia, India, Egypt, Nubia, and Ethiopia broke communion with the church of Constantinople and its patriarch. They did so without abandoning the heritage or tradition that the ecumenical patriarch represented, however. When the dust had finally settled, the ecumenical patriarch was unequivocally committed to the decisions reached at Chalcedon. Yet even the non-Chalcedonian communions looked back upon an earlier time when they had been in communion with him, representing an important historical memory of unity in their traditions. Constantinople and Orthodoxy were closely identified with one another among Christians east of the Dalmatian Coast in Europe, Asia, and Africa.

In 1204 armies of the Western crusaders who had set out mostly from Venice diverted from their intended destiny in the Holy Land to attack and sack Constantinople. The crusaders established one of their own Latin-speaking nobles as the new emperor of Constantinople. Ecumenical Patriarch John X fled to Thrace without renouncing his office. The crusaders established one of their own, however, a sub-deacon from Venice, as the new patriarch of Constantinople, a move which even Rome eventually came reluctantly to recognize. Meanwhile, members of the leading nobility in Constantinople went into exile in Nicaea, where they established the Empire of Nicaea under Theodore I Lascaris, a son-in-law of the previous emperor. Most of the Greek bishops fled as well to Nicaea. Theodore unsuccessfully sought to have Ecumenical Patriarch John X of Constantinople join him in Nicaea. When John died in 1206, Theodore appointed Michael IV as the next ecumenical patriarch of Constantinople, a move the other members of the Greek episcopacy who were with him in exile recognized. When Michael VIII Palaiologos, Emperor of Nicaea, took Constantinople in 1261 he formally reestablished the Byzantine Empire with himself as the emperor. He also brought with him Arsenios Autoreianos, who had been serving as ecumenical patriarch in Nicaea, reestablishing the Patriarchate in Constantinople. At that point the Patriarchate had survived nearly six decades of exile in Nicaea.

The year 1453 marked another turning point in the history of Constantinople: the army of the young Ottoman Sultan Mehmed II took the city and brought an end to the Byzantine Empire. A few days after securing control of the city Mehmed installed Gennadius Scholarius as the new ecumenical patriarch. The patriarch was made ruler of all the Greek (or Roman) *millet* ("subject nation") and *dhimmi* ("protected people"), a legally recognized but greatly restricted religious community within the Ottoman Empire. All Orthodox Christians residing within the Ottoman Empire were placed under the Roman *millet* and thus were subject to the ecumenical patriarch's political and religious oversight. The patriarch, in effect, became the ruler of a subjugated people under the control of the sultanate. Subsequent patriarchs would be elected only with the consent of sultans, who did not hesitate to interfere with the affairs of church life if they thought the interests of the empire were at stake. There was little alternative for the Greek Church leaders, as most of their people were now under Ottoman rule. The Empire of Trebizond, one of the Greek states that had emerged along the coast of the Black Sea following the crusaders' conquest of Constantinople in 1204, came under Ottoman control in 1461, ending the last Greek-speaking state that could provide the Ecumenical Patriarchate with a political home. The name of the city itself was changed from Constantinople to Istanbul.[2] The ecumenical patriarch was now an exile within his own historical city and homeland.

One of the striking aspects of this period of history in the Patriarchate is the fact that no one appears to have seriously considered removing the patriarchal office to a location that might have been more favorable to Christian life and administration outside the Ottoman Empire. It is more than a historical curiosity that no serious claimant to the Ecumenical Patriarchate emerged in exile. Despite considerable hardship and continuous persecution, successive patriarchs did not seek to leave Constantinople (or Istanbul). In doing so they maintained the historical continuity of the Patriarchate with its place, its location, on the other side of a massive shift in political and eventually cultural identity.

It could be argued that escape for the majority of church leaders in Constantinople in the immediate aftermath of events in 1453 was impossible, but this is only partially true. Some church leaders did leave, and there were ample opportunities for someone, perhaps with support from the West, to establish an alternative claimant to the throne from exile. The fact is that the majority of Orthodox Church leaders made the decision to stay and try to rebuild the church under their new Ottoman rulers. The decision was in part pastoral in nature. In the immediate aftermath of the fall of the city the majority of those whom the patriarch served in ministry were now living under Ottoman rule. The bishops and priests were organically related to these churches and would not have imagined living apart from them.

The largest body of Orthodox churches and believers outside Ottoman political domains at the time was in Russia, but relations between the majority of Russian church leaders and the Ecumenical Patriarchate were strained in 1453. In 1448, a mere five years before the Ottomans took Constantinople, the Russian Orthodox Church, largely in response to decisions made at the Council of Florence in 1445, had declared itself to be autocephalous under the metropolitan of Moscow. Ivan III succeeded in uniting the princes of the kingdom of Muscovy and bringing about Rus-

---

2. *Istanbul* is the Turkish version of a phrase that means "into the city" in Greek (*eis ton polin*) and was used by a number of non–Greek-speaking groups to identify Constantinople prior to the fifteenth century. The new name allowed the Ottomans to avoid calling the city *Constantinople,* which was identified with its Christian heritage.

sia's independence from Mongol rule several decades later in 1480. Ivan recognized the Russian Orthodox Church as fully autocephalous, and as the established religion of his state. Moscow now claimed to be the "Third Rome" and the proper inheritor of the ancient political mantle of Christendom.[3] The Ecumenical Patriarchate did not recognize the Russian claim to be autocephalous until more than a century later in 1589, when Jeremias II traveled to Moscow to participate in the service that elevated the metropolitan of Moscow to the ranks of a patriarch and installed the first occupant of that throne.

A number of Greek scholars made their way from Ottoman rule to other parts of Europe, where they took up residence and continued their work under Catholic Christian rulers in the sixteenth century. In Rome Pope Gregory XIII founded the Pontificio Collegio Greco to provide them with an intellectual home in which to work. The list of Greek scholars who eventually came to Western Europe is impressive. The future Patriarch Metrophanes III was still metropolitan of Caesarea (today known as Kayseri, Turkey) in the 1540s when he was sent by Patriarch Dionysius II to Venice and Rome in an unsuccessful effort to raise funds for the Patriarchate in Istanbul. Almost a century later Cyril Lukaris, who became Patriarch Cyril I, actually studied in the West and was accused by some of harboring Calvinist tendencies during his patriarchate. Clearly it was possible for Orthodox theology and the Orthodox Church to live outside its traditional Eastern territorial homeland, and to engage theologically the currents of thought that were coming from the West. I know of no effort or claim by any of these scholars or church leaders who either resided or traveled through Western Europe to have proposed moving the Patriarchate physically from Constantinople.

The relationship between Rome and Constantinople remained strained through the sixteenth and seventeenth centuries. Efforts by the Western church to achieve reunion on terms dictated by the Latin Church in earlier councils had generated considerable hostility among many in leadership in the Orthodox communion, and the memory of those events

---

3. The mantle in this case is literally a papal cowl. In the fourteenth century the legend took hold in Russia that the patriarch of Constantinople had been told in a dream to pass on to the archbishop of Novgorod (northern Russia) the white cowl that Constantine had supposedly given to Pope Sylvester in Rome, and which had been passed on in turn to Constantinople. In the sixteenth century the legendary dream came to undergird Moscow's claim to be the Third Rome, signified by the white cowl that the metropolitan, or later the patriarch of Moscow, wore.

continued to haunt the relationship between the two ancient sees. For many Orthodox Church leaders, the Western churches had departed theologically from the ancient tradition. Reports about the new movement in Germany to reform the Western churches had reached Constantinople at least by the 1550s, leading Patriarch Joasaph II to send a Serbian deacon named Demetrios Mysos to Wittenberg in 1559 to investigate. At Wittenberg Mysos met with Luther's younger colleague Philipp Melanchthon. One of the results of the Serbian deacon's visit was a translation of the Augsburg Confession into Greek. A copy of that translation along with letters from the Lutheran theologians in Tübingen was presented to Joasaph II's successor, Jeremias II, sometime after 1572 by Stephan Gerlach, the Lutheran chaplain to the German imperial ambassador to the sultan in Istanbul. An exchange of letters between the Orthodox patriarch and the Lutheran theologians ensued for several years. In the end disagreements over matters such as the doctrine of justification, the number of sacraments, the role of saints and of icons, and the infallibility of Tradition kept the two sides apart.

Several years later Patriarch Jeremias II rejected Gregory XIII's proposal to adopt a reformed common calendar, but sent several relics to Rome as a gift. The correspondence led to Jeremias's arrest, which was supported by some of the others in leadership in the Greek Church on the basis of their suspicion that he was colluding with Rome. French diplomats to the sultanate eventually secured his release. Following his release Jeremias traveled through Poland to Russia, where in 1589 he participated in the consecration of Job as the first patriarch of Moscow and All of Russia. Jeremias made the journey to Russia in part to secure funds from the Russian government to help support the Orthodox churches in the Ottoman world. By some accounts he was considered as a candidate for the Patriarch of Moscow, but declined. He returned to Istanbul, where he died in 1595.

The Ottoman Empire traded with the Christian nations to its north and west, regularly bringing Christian merchants, and along with them Western Christian church leaders (first as chaplains, later as missionaries) into Ottoman territories. Most of the merchants in the Ottoman Empire were Muslims, but a small number were Greeks. During the seventeenth century the wealth among these Greek merchant families, who were called "Phanariotes," after the district of Phanar where most of them resided after 1599, increased considerably. Contacts with European powers increased considerably through the seventeenth and eighteenth centuries as well. The growing strength of European nations within the Ottoman Empire resulted in increased privileges for foreigners residing within its territories. For several centuries the Ottomans had been granting rights to foreign citizens within its territories under what were called "capitulations." France and Russia in particular claimed under their capitulations to have the right to oversee religious affairs of Catholic and Orthodox Christians within the Ottoman realms. Roman Catholic missionaries operated within the Ottoman Empire mostly under these capitulations. Their converts came mainly from various Orthodox communions, such as the Armenian, Coptic, or Greek churches. In the eighteenth century a number of Orthodox churches entered into uniate agreements with Rome that allowed them to maintain their Orthodox theology and liturgy while recognizing the universal pastoral office of the bishop of Rome, thereby entering into full communion with Rome and departing from communion with the ecumenical patriarch. The Ecumenical Patriarchate became embroiled in constant controversies not only with its Ottoman rulers, but now with other Christian communions and even with its own churches within its own historical territories. The experience of the patriarch being exiled within his own homeland only increased.

The nineteenth century was particularly turbulent for the Ecumenical Patriarchate. The Ottoman Empire was in decline as a political power, and a number of independence movements were emerging throughout its territories. In 1821 fighting broke out in several locations in Greece as nationalists launched a revolution. In Istanbul, Patriarch Gregory V condemned the Greek independence movement, but that did not stop the sultan from having him hanged on Easter Sunday following the high liturgy in retaliation for the death of Muslims at the hands of Greek revolutionaries. Fighting continued for a decade but eventually, under pressure from the combined governments of France, Russia, and the United Kingdom, Greece was granted its independence by the Ottoman rulers in 1832 under terms of the Treaty of Constantinople. The first ruler of the newly independent nation was an underage Bavarian prince named Otto, who was a Roman Catholic. With the support of the Bavarian regents who ruled in Otto's name, the Orthodox bishops in Greece in 1833 gathered in a synod and declared themselves to be an autocephalous church under the administrative oversight of the archbishop of Athens. The ecumenical patriarch continued to be regarded as a spiritual authority by the Greek Church, and to exercise administrative oversight of the churches in the northern region as well as in several islands in the Aegean Sea and in Crete, but by 1850 the patriarch had to acknowledge that the main church of Greece was now autocephalous.

Other movements toward autocephaly ensued throughout various regions of Eastern Europe that had historically been under Ottoman rule. In Bulgaria, a nationalist movement emerged under the Ottoman rulers that expressed itself first as a challenge to the authority of the Greek bishops and the patriarchate as being the head of their *millet* community. The sultan sided with the Bulgarian nationalists and in 1870 recognized the Bulgarian-speaking churches within the Ottoman Empire to be an autocephalous communion with its own bishop in Constantinople. The Holy Synod under Patriarch Anthimus VI condemned the decision and declared the Bulgarian Church to be in schism, but it mattered little. The division lasted until well into the twentieth century, until the patriarchate finally recognized the Bulgarian Church as autocephalous. One of the results of the movement toward autocephaly was to place greater emphasis within the life of the various autocephalous churches upon their separate and distinct ethnic identities, and to increase the sense of being local or regional ethnic communions, in contrast to the "ecumenical" character and meaning of the patriarchate in Constantinople.

The year 1923 brought a major change in the status of the Ecumenical Patriarchate, as the Ottoman Empire came to an official end and the secular Republic of Turkey emerged to take its political place. The patriarchate continued to face significant political challenges within the new republic, as noted earlier. The ecumenical patriarch was only recognized by the Turkish government as being the head of the minority religious community of ethnic Greeks who were members of the Orthodox Church within Turkey. The Turkish government still today does not recognize the title of ecumenical patriarch.[4] For his part the patriarch exercises administrative oversight of the Greek Orthodox churches in Turkey, parts of Greece, Crete, Mount Athos, and in various lands in North America and Asia where Greek Orthodox have immigrated. The administrative functions of the pastoral office are considerably reduced from what they were as late as the nineteenth century.

As the administrative functions of the office have decreased, however,

---

4. According to the Orthodox Church, the full title is His All Holiness, Bartholomew I, Archbishop of Constantinople New Rome and Ecumenical Patriarch. According to the Turkish government, his title is Bartholomew I, Patriarch of the Fener Greek Orthodox Patriarchate in Istanbul.

the spiritual importance and even impact of the Ecumenical Patriarchate within the wider community of world Christianity have increased. The most notable expression of this is seen in the role that the patriarch has played in the twentieth-century ecumenical movement, extending both the visibility and the impact of the office considerably among the various Orthodox bodies who have not shared communion for a millennium, and with both Roman Catholic and ecumenical dialogue partners. A subtle shift in emphasis from "patriarch" to "ecumenical" in his title has taken place over the course of the twentieth century as a result. Bartholomew has pointed out on occasion the significance of the fact that the patriarchate of Constantinople was most likely the first Christian institution to be called "ecumenical," beginning perhaps as early as the fourth century.[5] He is only following the lead of his predecessors in the office since the beginning of the twentieth century, however, in pointing toward this renewed sense of the patriarch's ecumenical role.

The possibility of healing the historical divisions among Christian communions had been cautiously broached in 1902 in an encyclical by Patriarch Joachim III that was addressed to the other Orthodox churches that had sent greetings on the occasion of his elevation for the second time to the patriarchal throne. Joachim celebrated the mutual love and unity that existed among the Orthodox despite historical differences and divisions in language and nationality among them. He called for a pan-Orthodox conference and extended this vision and hope to Roman Catholics and Protestants in the West. Union of all who believe in Christ within the Orthodox Church was the heartfelt desire of all Orthodox Christians, he noted. The main obstacle to expressing such unity was Protestant and Roman Catholic insistence on holding doctrines that were unacceptable to the Orthodox.[6] Joachim saw some hope for further conversations with Old Catholics who had separated from Rome after 1871 and the promulgation of the doctrine of papal infallibility, and Anglicans. His ecumenical vision was beginning to extend the patriarch's role in new directions.

The major milestone that marked this shift in emphasis and the opening of a new period of ecumenical life in the churches throughout the

5. See Bartholomew, Ecumenical Patriarch of Constantinople, *In the World, Yet Not of the World: Social and Global Initiatives of Ecumenical Patriarch Bartholomew,* ed. John Chryssavgis (New York: Fordham University Press, 2010), 78.

6. "Patriarchal and Synodical Encyclical of 1902," in *The Orthodox Church in the Ecumenical Movement: Documents and Statements, 1902-1975,* ed. Constantin G. Patelos (Geneva: WCC, 1978), 30.

world was the encyclical letter "Unto the Churches of Christ Everywhere," issued at the beginning of 1920 by the Ecumenical Patriarchate. The actual office of the patriarch was vacant at the time that the encyclical was written, causing it to be published by the Holy Synod under the authority of the Patriarchate. Germanos Strenopoulos, who had studied in the West and had become personally acquainted with leading figures of the emerging ecumenical movement among Protestants and Anglicans, and who would later serve as archbishop of the Greek Orthodox archdiocese of Thyatira and Great Britain, is usually credited with being the major influence upon the text.[7] "Unto the Churches of Christ Everywhere" called for rapprochement and fellowship among all Christian churches throughout the world, to overcome the mutual distrust, bitterness, enmity, and even hatred that had arisen among them, and especially to end the practice of proselytism that was disturbing the churches especially in the East. The encyclical outlined a number of mutual concrete steps that could be taken by churches throughout the world, including agreement upon a common calendar, exchange of letters of mutual support, exchanges in theological schools, holding pan-Christian conferences for study of doctrinal issues, addressing pastoral concerns regarding mixed marriages and use of burial grounds, and common social action. In order to further these ends the encyclical famously called for a "league" or "fellowship" (*koinonia* in Greek) of churches that would be formed along the lines of the newly formed League of Nations.[8]

The history of the Orthodox involvement and leadership in the ecumenical movement in the twentieth century is well known and amply documented, enough so to forgo its retelling here.[9] Suffice it to say that the

---

7. The claim is made by Willem A. Visser 't Hooft in *The Genesis and Formation of the World Council of Churches* (Geneva: WCC, 1982), 2. For a full consideration of the importance of Archbishop Germanos Strenopoulos in the twentieth-century ecumenical movement, see Vasil T. Istavridis, "The Work of Germanos Strenopoulos in the Field of Inter-Orthodox and Inter-Christian Relations," *Ecumenical Review* 11, no. 3 (1959): 291-299.

8. For the full text of the encyclical see Michael Kinnamon and Brian E. Cope, eds., *The Ecumenical Movement: An Anthology of Key Texts and Voices* (Geneva: WCC, 1997), 11-14.

9. The bibliography related to the Orthodox participation in the ecumenical movement is too extensive to rehearse here, but two basic introductions are Nicolas Zernov, "The Eastern Churches and the Ecumenical Movement in the Twentieth Century," in *A History of the Ecumenical Movement,* ed. Ruth Rouse and Stephen Charles Neill (Geneva: WCC, 1948), 649-654; and Vasil T. Istavridis, "The Orthodox Churches in the Ecumenical Movement, 1948-1968," in *The Ecumenical Advance: A History of the Ecumenical Movement,* vol. 2: *1948-1968,* ed. Harold E. Fey (Geneva: WCC, 1986), 297-307.

conversation has not been entirely without difficulties as well as major breakthroughs in understanding. Orthodox participants in the ecumenical movement have not wavered from their understanding that there is One Undivided Unbroken Holy Tradition of the Church of Christ, and that this Holy Tradition is fully identified with and embodied by the Orthodox Church. The Church is not divided, Orthodox participants in ecumenical dialogue constantly remind their interlocutors from other communions. There are some who call themselves Christian who are nevertheless separated from the True Church. "In Orthodoxy, one can find not only the correct faith in the true God but also the correct perception of man [*sic*] as the image of God, of the world, and of creation," notes Bartholomew.[10]

Among the Orthodox themselves there has been considerable controversy and tension over the participation of Orthodox Church leaders and teachers in the ecumenical movement. One need only surf the Orthodox web pages on the internet to see such objections and hostile responses, often amounting to charges of heresy against the ecumenical patriarch and others within the Orthodox communion who have supported the ecumenical movement through the course of the century. Often such opposition comes from quarters that represent national or cultural expressions of Orthodoxy, or from individuals who are converts from more conservative Protestant evangelical traditions. But this is not always the case. The criticism leveled against the Ecumenical Patriarchate from monks on Mount Athos in response to the joint Catholic-Orthodox Balamand Statement of 1993 is such an example.[11] For the authors of the statement Roman Catholicism is a heresy. Any concession that it is a sister church sharing the same holy Tradition in the past is a concession to heresy.

Bartholomew has chosen to respond to such vitriolic criticisms of his involvement in ecumenical life by engaging further, by deepening his commitment and the commitment of the Patriarchate to such efforts. He has sought to emphasize the ecumenical nature of his office, in other words, not just on behalf of the Orthodox, but on behalf of all in the world who seek to follow Christ, however falteringly such efforts on the part of Protestants and Catholics may appear to the Orthodox to be. In doing so Bartholomew has consistently looked not only to the past, to the Great and

10. Bartholomew, *In the World, Yet Not of the World,* 20.

11. See "Letter to the Ecumenical Patriarch Concerning the Balamand Agreement," posted on the web page of the Orthodox Christian Information Center, a particularly strong anti-ecumenical Orthodox web site. Available online at http://orthoxinfo.com/ecumenism/athos_bal.aspx.

Holy Tradition that he unquestionably understands the Orthodox Church to be. He is also looking consistently and unwaveringly across the divides of world Christianity to other communions and traditions, and to the future, as he noted in his plenary address before the Faith and Order Commission in 2009 that was quoted at the opening of this essay.[12]

Bartholomew's response to his critics inside the Orthodox communion, like his ecumenical leadership in general, has been one that is steeped in humility. Furthermore, he has chosen to make his response and exercise ecumenical leadership self-consciously not only from a place of humility, but from a location on the margins. Bartholomew perhaps more than any of his predecessors in the Patriarchate has become a world-figure. He has done so with a spirit of humility that expresses the power of the gospel in profoundly new ways. As patriarch he is not afraid to recall the heritage of Constantine the Great and the long history of imperial Christianity that is in part the heritage of Byzantium. He knows well how Orthodoxy functioned as the soul of the empire, holding it together and empowering it with a transcendental vision that reached far beyond the walls of Constantinople and the territories its armies could control. He also knows that in an important sense the end of the Byzantine Empire in 1453 freed the ecumenical patriarch from historical burdens of imperial Christendom and being an imperial church. Nothing was lost in terms of the church's self-understanding of transcendence, and of having preserved in unadulterated form through the ages the ancient tradition of Christian faith.[13] Much has been gained, however, in understanding how the true power of Orthodox faith comes not from "worldly structures of power and authority" but from love.[14]

The expression and exercise of power, be it economic or political, in the life of the Patriarchate has clearly changed. The relationship between

12. See the speeches published in chapter 1, "The Ecumenical Patriarch: Visionary Ministry," in Bartholomew, *In the World, Yet Not of the World*, 15-31.

13. See Bartholomew, Ecumenical Patriarch of Constantinople, *Encountering the Mystery: Understanding Orthodox Christianity Today* (New York: Doubleday, 2008), xli, 38-40.

14. Concerning globalization and the material economic power that it generates, Bartholomew writes in *Encountering the Mystery*, 159: "While it is true that the Orthodox Church invites all people to one faith, its love for all people is never contingent upon adherence to this faith. Moreover, the ecumenicity of our faith is not related to worldly structures of power and authority. From this point of view, then, the ecumenicity of the Orthodox Church, and in particular of the Ecumenical Patriarchate within the worldwide Orthodox Church, differs substantially from the recent phenomenon of economic globalization."

patriarchs and emperors in Constantinople prior to 1453 was historically always complex, and at times contentious, but it resulted in considerable mixing of spiritual and material forms of power. While emperors did not have formal ecclesiastical standing, this did not stop them from interfering at times in matters pertaining to faith and order in the church. Emperors often used their considerable political power to influence the selection of patriarchs, and patriarchs could hardly survive without imperial support. For their part, however, patriarchs exercised spiritual authority over emperors, and at times used it to excommunicate emperors for actions that were considered flagrantly immoral or that violated canons of church law. Patriarchs could also exercise administrative power within the political realm of the Byzantine Empire, often making them significant political players in the drama of Byzantine imperial life. The Ottomans transferred imperial authority over the church to the sultan. They continued to exercise considerable political power over ecclesiastical affairs, primarily through the appointment (and often deposition) of the patriarch.

Willem A. Visser 't Hooft, the first General Secretary of the World Council of Churches, argued that the collapse of the Byzantine Empire removed the political overtones of ecumenicity for the Patriarchate.[15] John Meyendorff, on the other hand, argued that while the Ottoman conquest of Constantinople brought about a change in the political character of the ecumenical patriarch, it did not entirely remove all political overtones.[16] The patriarchate under the Ottoman rulers was invested with an even greater degree of political power than it had exercised under the Byzantine emperors as the head of a subjugated *millet* nation, Meyendorff notes. That power was limited as the Ottomans had effectively cut off the patriarch from exercising authority in other parts of the Christian world. The rise of autocephalous churches in former Ottoman territories in the nineteenth century reduced even further the administrative reach of the ecumenical patriarch. The Ecumenical Patriarchate has come to be divested of its political overtones most fully in the twentieth century under Turkish law, allowing it to realize its fuller ecumenical meaning in powerlessness.

Bartholomew has come to embrace this political weakness and its attending economic poverty as a strength. As Olivier Clément notes,

15. W. A. Visser 't Hooft, "The Word 'Ecumenical': Its History and Use," in *A History of the Ecumenical Movement, 1517-1948*, ed. Ruth Rouse, Stephen Neill, and Harold E. Fey (Geneva: WCC, 1986), 737.

16. John Meyendorff, *The Orthodox Church: Its Past and Its Role in the World Today* (Crestwood, NY: St. Vladimir's Seminary Press, 1981), 88.

Constantinople's weakness on the material plane, its poverty, ensures its impartiality and, paradoxically, increases its prestige. The ecumenical patriarch has no pretensions to be a "universal bishop." He claims no dogmatic infallibility, no direct jurisdiction over all the faithful. He has no temporal powers. As a center of appeal whose aim is to preserve the faith and the unity of all, his primacy consists not in power, but in sacrificial offering of service, in imitation of the One who came not to be served but to serve.[17]

Moreover, the Patriarch has linked powerlessness with marginality and exile. In numerous instances in his many speeches and interviews the patriarch has located himself and his office in a place that is marginal to world Christian life, marginal to globalization as it is dominated by the West, and marginal to the dominant cultural (but not spiritual) heritage of Western Christendom.[18] And it is precisely from this marginal location, which can even be called exilic, that the Patriarch is able to exercise most fully his ecumenical ministry. This is so because for Bartholomew, life on the margin allows one to be a bridge.[19] The image of patriarch as bridge builder and the Patriarchate itself as bridge shows up repeatedly in Bartholomew's ministry. One of the bridges he has worked to build is among Orthodox of different communions, including the non-Chalcedonians. Another has been the bridge with Protestants and Catholics in the ecumenical movement. A third has been the political and cultural bridge between East and West, between Europe and Asia. A fourth has been a bridge among Judaism, Christianity, and Islam as Abrahamic faiths. Running through these efforts is a common theme that shifts the role of the patriarch from being at the center of any particular empire or nation to being a bridge among empires and nations. The patriarchate is in service to the "commonwealth" (think koinonia) of all.[20]

These are not just empty conversations. The patriarch has convened a

---

17. Olivier Clément, *Conversations with Ecumenical Patriarch Bartholomew I,* trans. Paul Meyendorff (Crestwood, NY: St. Vladimir's Seminary Press, 1997), 31-32.

18. In addresses to a conference of chief executive officers and NATO representatives in Istanbul in 2005 and 2006, published in *In the World, Yet Not of the World,* Bartholomew called the "legacy of the Eastern Roman Empire" a missing link and perhaps the "best-kept secret in the West." "The West has never truly acknowledged its debt to Byzantium," he notes (47).

19. See "The Patriarch as Bridge Builder," in Bartholomew, *Encountering the Mystery,* xxxiv-xlii.

20. Clément, *Conversations with Ecumenical Patriarch Bartholomew,* 138.

number of important gatherings, attended numerous conferences, and visited numerous other nations in a continuing effort to build new bridges of peace and understanding. The range of his work has been profound. He has addressed globalization and global economic inequalities, the Holocaust, the more recent genocide in Rwanda, the global AIDS epidemic, racism and terrorism, Turkey's place in the European community, and of course the global environmental crisis. This hardly begins to touch on the social, political, economic, and cultural issues he has addressed. But he has been equally a figure of profound spiritual insight and commitment. Always he has shown himself to be motivated and guided by deep spiritual insight. Indeed, it is from these spiritual depths that his sense of powerlessness and marginality ultimately derives. Bartholomew himself has noted the significance of the apophatic attitude and the tradition of negative theology in the East in this regard. "Negative theology, therefore, is not merely a corrective or corresponding way to the affirming approach," he notes. "It is the only way to God."[21]

Bartholomew writes of these things, of the mystery, of the apophatic tradition, of unity, of humility, and of the "turning" toward the past and future in conversion in the end to help us cross the bridge between humanity and divinity that Christ is, that continues to be found in the Church that lives in the Spirit, and that we cross each time we enter into worship. In one of his most poignant and insightful paragraphs the patriarch writes:

> Each evening, as I shut the door to my office, I do not leave behind the people and issues that I have faced during that day. I bring them with me and within my heart to the small Patriarchal Chapel, where they are all offered in prayer during the Compline service that closes the day. The chapel is a small refuge from the daily deluge of problems, a splendid occasion to meditate on the wonders of God, who loves us as we are. What more could I ever ask for? What more could I ever do?[22]

I for one am thankful to have the Patriarch carry on my behalf my concerns and indeed world into that chapel in prayer.

---

21. Bartholomew, *Encountering the Mystery,* 53.
22. Bartholomew, *Encountering the Mystery,* 36.

CHAPTER 5

Patriarch Bartholomew as a Leader in Orthodox-Catholic Dialogue

Ronald G. Roberson, CSP

In his enthronement address on 2 November 1991, newly elected Ecumenical Patriarch Bartholomew reflected not only on his role among Orthodox churches, but also on relations with other churches and religions. Turning to the Catholic Church, he had this to say:

> From this sacred courtyard, we also greet His Holiness the Pope of Elder Rome, John Paul II, with whom we are in a communion of love. We assure him that a very serious concern for us will be the realization of the sacred vision of our late predecessors, Athenagoras and Demetrios, in order that the way of the Lord may be fulfilled on earth for His holy Church in the reunion of all those who believe in Him through the dialogue of truth. We shall do everything in our power to move in this direction, with fear of God, sincerity, honesty, and prudence. We are convinced that our brother in the West will exhaust all the many possibilities at his disposal in order to cooperate with us in this sacred and holy objective.[1]

1. Enthronement Address of His All Holiness, Ecumenical Patriarch Bartholomew I, available online at http://www.patriarchate.org/documents/1991-enthronement-address. Accessed 5 August 2011.

Dedicated to His Eminence William Cardinal Keeler, Archbishop Emeritus of Baltimore. The Cardinal served for many years as a member of the international Orthodox-Catholic dialogue, and hosted its plenary meeting in Emmitsburg, Maryland, in 2000. In 1997 Cardinal Keeler warmly welcomed Patriarch Bartholomew to a series of events in Baltimore, including a prayer service in the Basilica of the Assumption and a dinner in his personal residence.

The new Patriarch was thus placing himself within his church's well-established tradition of efforts to promote Christian unity, efforts that go back to the beginning of the twentieth century. Patriarch Joachim III's encyclicals of 1902 and 1904 encouraged theological engagement with Western Christianity. In 1920 Patriarch Meletios IV addressed an encyclical to all the Christian churches, calling for unity. The Ecumenical Patriarchate would also be among the founding members of the World Council of Churches in 1948.

Prelude: The Early Years of Dialogue with the Catholic Church

Patriarch Athenagoras (1886-1972, patriarch from 1948) began to focus more precisely on relations with the Catholic Church, and initiated a process that contributed to a gradual rapprochement between the two churches. On the Catholic side, the documents of the Second Vatican Council (1962-1965) included a positive attitude towards Orthodox transitions and expressed a desire to engage in dialogue. The third Pan-Orthodox Conference on Rhodes in 1964 encouraged the local Orthodox churches to prepare for a full-scale dialogue with Rome. These events paved the way for dramatic gestures in the following years that included a historic meeting between Patriarch Athenagoras and Pope Paul VI in Jerusalem in 1965, and the formal lifting of the excommunications of 1054 in Rome and Istanbul on 6 December 1965. These gestures constituted what would be called the "dialogue of charity" between the two communions, a dialogue that was intended to increase trust between the two churches as they prepared for an eventual theological dialogue.[2]

It was only in 1976 that a joint commission was established to assess the prospects of a formal theological engagement. In 1978 it presented the authorities of both churches with a program that defined the goal of a future dialogue as the establishment of full communion. It proposed that the dialogue begin with areas Catholics and Orthodox have in common, specifically the sacraments and their relationship to ecclesiology.

A year later, in November 1979, during a visit by Pope John Paul II to

---

2. For correspondence and other documentation from this period, see E. J. Stormon, S.J., ed., *Towards the Healing of Schism: The Sees of Rome and Constantinople; Public Statements and Correspondence between the Holy See and the Ecumenical Patriarchate, 1958-1984* (New York: Paulist Press, 1987).

Patriarch Demetrios (1914-1991, patriarch from 1972) in Istanbul, the heads of the two churches formally announced the establishment of the "Joint International Commission for Theological Dialogue between the Catholic Church and the Orthodox Church." It met for the first time on the islands of Patmos and Rhodes in 1980, and made substantial progress for ten years. In Munich in 1982, the commission adopted a common text, "The Mystery of the Church and of the Eucharist in the Light of the Mystery of the Holy Trinity." In Bari, Italy, in 1987 the dialogue finalized another agreed statement, "Faith, Sacraments, and the Unity of the Church." At the Orthodox monastery in Valamo, Finland, in 1988, the commission adopted a joint document, "The Sacrament of Order in the Sacramental Structure of the Church, with Particular Reference to the Importance of the Apostolic Succession for the Sanctification and Unity of the People of God."[3] At Valamo the members also agreed on a topic for the dialogue's next phase: "Ecclesiological and Canonical Consequences of the Sacramental Structure of the Church: Conciliarity and Authority in the Church."

However, the very encouraging progress made during these first ten years of dialogue came to an abrupt end almost immediately after the Valamo meeting. Cracks were already beginning to appear in the Soviet monolith in Central and Eastern Europe, and only a year later the Communist regimes in the area began to collapse one after another. In these new conditions of freedom, Eastern Catholic Churches in the region began to reemerge after decades of persecution by the Communist authorities, and to demand the return of the churches that had been taken from them and given over to the Orthodox decades earlier. For their part, the Orthodox feared a resurgence of a militant form of Catholic proselytism that they had experienced in past centuries and which had contributed to the formation of some of these Eastern Catholic Churches. These long-dormant anxieties, coupled with a general lack of knowledge about recent improvements in Orthodox-Catholic relations, set the stage for a major confrontation between the two churches in that part of the world.[4]

All of this colored the atmosphere when the members of the international dialogue gathered in Freising, Germany, in June 1990. At the request of the Orthodox side, the draft text on conciliarity and authority that had

3. All these agreed statements can be found in J. Borelli and J. Erickson, eds., *The Quest for Unity: Orthodox and Catholics in Dialogue* (Crestwood, NY: St. Vladimir's Seminary Press, 1996).

4. See Ronald Roberson, "The Revolutions of 1989 and the Catholic-Orthodox Dialogue," *Christian Orient* 13 (1992): 195-211.

been prepared for the meeting was set aside, and the members focused their attention exclusively on the volatile situation in Eastern Europe. The meeting concluded with the adoption of a rather brief statement which acknowledged the seriousness of the situation and called for a full-scale analysis of a range of issues related to the origins and present role of the Eastern Catholic Churches.[5]

It was at this critical juncture in the dialogue's history that Patriarch Demetrios died on 2 October 1991. Twenty days later, on 22 October, Metropolitan Bartholomew of Chalcedon was elected as his successor. The speech he gave at his enthronization revealed his respect and esteem for the Catholic Church in spite of the new problems. Indeed, Bartholomew had a familiarity with the Catholic Church that would serve him well in his new role.

Patriarch Bartholomew: Early Experiences of the Catholic Church

In fact, Deacon Bartholomew Archondonis had arrived in Rome in 1963, at the age of twenty-three, with a scholarship from the Ecumenical Patriarchate and the recommendation of Metropolitan Maximos of Stavropoulos to study canon law at the Pontifical Oriental Institute. The Second Vatican Council was still in progress and the Secretariat for Promoting Christian Unity, at that time still a temporary structure of the Council, was able to place him at the French College in Rome's historic center. Monsignor Johannes Willebrands and Father Pierre Duprey of the staff of the Secretariat looked after the young deacon the next few years as he pursued his studies not only in Rome but also at the Ecumenical Institute in Bossey, Switzerland, then under the direction of the Greek Orthodox theologian Nikos Nissiotis (1935-1986), and at the University of Munich, where he learned German and studied the theology of Karl Rahner and Joseph Ratzinger.[6]

During these years Bartholomew gained extensive knowledge of the main currents in contemporary Catholic theology. Even though he was not an official observer at the Council, he no doubt took part in many of the

---

5. "Sixth Plenary Meeting of the Joint International Commission for Theological Dialogue between the Roman Catholic Church and the Orthodox Church," *Information Service* 73, no. 2 (1990): 52-53.

6. John Chryssavgis, "Biographical Note," in Bartholomew, Ecumenical Patriarch of Constantinople, *Encountering the Mystery: Understanding Orthodox Christianity Today* (New York: Doubleday, 2008), xxviii-xxix.

discussions behind the scenes. He would also serve as one of the four members of the joint commission that prepared the publication of the *Τόμος Αγάπης*, the volume that documented relations between the Vatican and the Ecumenical Patriarchate from 1958 until 1970.[7]

Bartholomew received his doctorate in 1968, defending his thesis on 21 December of that year. The thesis was entitled "The Codification of the Holy Canons and the Canonical Constitution of the Orthodox Church." Because the Pontifical Oriental Institute was not able at that time to grant degrees in Canon Law, the doctorate was awarded by the Pontifical Gregorian University, with which the Oriental Institute is associated.

Years later, Patriarch Bartholomew reflected on his time in Rome. On 10 March 2011, the Patriarch received a group of students at the Ecumenical Patriarchate who were visiting from the Institute of St. Apolinarius in Rome. In his address to the students, he described his years in Rome at the Pontifical Oriental Institute as among the most significant experiences of his life.[8]

In April 2011 the Patriarch was in Paris for the presentation of the French version of his book *Encountering the Mystery.* In his preface to the French edition, Bartholomew wrote about his vivid memories of the years he lived at the French College in Rome:

> A young cleric of the Ecumenical Patriarchate of Greek origin, an Orthodox on Roman and Catholic turf, who was also learning French, had not been seen for centuries. In addition to learning the chant, we also studied the great French Catholic theologians. All of us are indebted to Jean Danielou, Henri de Lubac and Yves Conger, whose teaching influenced theology well beyond Catholicism, and touched more broadly on the entire theological renewal of the twentieth century.[9]

7. *Τόμος Αγάπης: Vatican-Phanar (1958-1970)* (Rome and Istanbul, 1971). The other members of the commission were Archimandrite Damaskino Papandreou, Fr. Pierre Duprey, and Fr. Christophe Dumont.

8. "Fate quello che dice il Papa," *L'Osservatore Romano,* 16 March 2011, 6: ". . . una delle principali e significative esperienze della propria essistenza."

9. "La Francia e il cristianesmo ortodosso. Nella prefazione di un libro del Patriarca ecumenico di Constantinopoli," *L'Osservatore Romano,* 13 April 2011, 6. "Un giovane chierico del Patriarcato ecumenico, di origine greca, ortodosso in terra romana e cattolica, che per giunta imparava il francese, non si vedeva da secoli. All'apprendimento dei canti, aggiungevamo lo studio dei grandi teologi cattolici francesi. Siamo tutti in debito con Jean Daniélou, Henri de Lubac e Yves Congar, il cui insegnamento segnò la teologia ben al di là del solo cattolicesimo e toccò più largamente tutto il rinnovamento teologico del XX secolo."

The Patriarch went on to describe his several visits to France since his election, and wrote that he had maintained "close links with the culture, the art, but also the intellectual and theological life of France." He recalled that in 1995, during his first visit to France after his election, he had addressed the Catholic bishops of France, stressing the importance of ecumenical dialogue for the recovery of Christian unity.

Cardinal Edward Cassidy, then president of the Pontifical Council for Promoting Christian Unity, referred to this background in his remarks to Vatican Radio immediately after Bartholomew's election. He recalled that the new patriarch "studied in Rome at the Gregorian University; he had contacts with the then Secretariat and now Pontifical Council on many occasions. We can say that he is a good friend of our Pontifical Council."[10] As patriarch, Bartholomew would head the Ecumenical Patriarchate's delegation to Rome for the feast of Sts. Peter and Paul in June 1995, 2004, and 2008, sign a common declaration on the environment with Pope John Paul II in 2002, receive Pope Benedict XVI at Phanar in November 2006, and in 2008 visit the Pontifical Oriental Institute on its ninetieth anniversary and address the Synod of Bishops in Rome. In 1994 Pope John Paul II had invited the Patriarch to contribute the traditional meditations that are read out during the Pope's celebration of the Way of the Cross at the Coliseum on Good Friday.[11]

Spokesman for Orthodoxy

In his role as Ecumenical Patriarch, however, Bartholomew has never allowed these warm contacts with Catholics going back to his student days to lessen his Orthodox convictions. In his statement to the Holy Synod on 24 October 1991, immediately after his election and before his enthronization, Bartholomew had said that even though he intended to foster dialogue among Christians in the hope of achieving unity, he would "never hesitate to condemn or severely criticize injustices or plans against the Orthodox Church, just as I have always done in the past."[12]

10. Perduto, Giovanni, "Il nuovo patriarca ecumenico di Constantinopoli," Radio Vaticana Radiogiornale, 23 October 1991.

11. "The Via Crucis: Common Witness of Pope and Patriarch; Good Friday 1994," *Information Service* 86, no. 2-3 (1994): 112-124.

12. "Déclarations du nouveau Patriarche devant le Saint-Synode Endémoussa," *Episkepsis* 469 (October 1991): 8: "Cela ne signifie pas que j'hésiterai à condemner ou à

Indeed, the Patriarch sees one of his primary roles among the Orthodox churches as giving voice to the common concerns of Orthodoxy as a whole.[13]

The combination of a strong defense of Orthodoxy and commitment to ecumenical dialogue with other Christians has played itself out in the Patriarch's relations with the Catholic Church in various ways. Commenting on the new *Catechism of the Catholic Church* in 1993,[14] for example, the Patriarch praises the document on a number of points, including its description of the human person as made in the image of God, and of grace as participation in the life of God, both eminently consistent with Eastern Christian anthropology. He also lauds its presentation of the Church as the mystery of Christ, as a Eucharistic community gathered in the power of the Spirit. He is particularly pleased that it cites the complete text of the Creed of the Seventh Ecumenical Council, which he interprets as a long-overdue full and true reception of that council by the Latin Church. Other positive elements include its portrayal of the priest at the Eucharist as making present, in the Spirit, the one sacrifice of Christ, its affirmation that the entire community celebrates the Eucharist together, and the importance of the epiclesis. He also appreciates the Catechism's placement of history within the eschatological perspective and, contrary to any superficial progressive understanding of history, its statement that since God's Kingdom will come about through the Church's death and resurrection, we need not expect a triumph of the Church in history. He also praises the way in which the document deals with the life of prayer, and its portrayal of Mary as the perfect example of the prayerful Christian.

But the Patriarch does not hesitate to criticize the Catechism on a number of points. He feels that the document's treatment of scientific and theological understandings of the origins of the world and of evil "remains precarious and uncertain." On eschatology, Bartholomew asks if it was necessary simply to repeat what he calls the fundamentally individualistic formulas of the fourteenth century without criticism or nuance. "If in dying and being judged in a particular way some find themselves definitively in hell and others contemplating the divine 'essence' what would be left of

critiquer sévèrement les injustices et visées au dépens de l'Eglise orthodoxe, comme je l'ai déjà fait dans le passé."

13. Luigi Geninazzi, "Un ponte da Costantinopoli: Parla il patriarca Bartolomeo all' vigilia del Sinodo ortodosso," *Avvenire,* 11 March 1992, 3.

14. Gianni Valente, "The Essential That Unites," *30 Days,* April 1993, 22-26.

the communion of the saints and the parousia? Why is there no talk of the hope and prayer for universal salvation found in St. Ambrose, Gregory of Nyssa," and others. "These are fundamental problems for today's man who oscillates tragically between the anguish of nothingness and the false promises of reincarnation."

Turning to the Catechism's treatment of ecclesiology, the Ecumenical Patriarch finds that differences emerge most sharply in the way it deals with the role of the pope in the Church. He acknowledges that during the first millennium "the East recognized the ministry of Rome," and that Vatican II "rediscovered the importance of the Episcopal College. But from the Gregorian Reform to the First Vatican Council, the diakonia of Rome became absolute power and Vatican II did not dare establish true interdependence between pope and bishops." When asked about the Catechism's treatment of the *filioque* problem, the Patriarch remarked that the presentation was "somewhat confusing," and questionable from an Orthodox point of view. The text simply repeats the affirmations of the Council of Florence, which were almost immediately rejected by the Orthodox bishops and faithful. He lamented the fact that the Catechism does not take into account the efforts of Orthodox and Catholic theologians in recent decades to find a solution to this problem. He believes that we are dealing with two pneumatologies which may complement one another as long as one does not try to absorb the other. "I am not sure that Catholic leaders are paying enough attention to this question today," he concluded.

When asked about the treatment of marriage and clerical celibacy in the Catechism, the Patriarch responded that one should not overemphasize the disciplinary differences between the two churches. He said that Catholics and Orthodox teaching on the ideal of marriage is the same, but Orthodoxy has a certain "economy" that does not admit but forgives divorce in some cases. On the matter of priestly celibacy, the Patriarch notes that while the Catechism states that the Eastern churches have had the tradition of married priests "for centuries," in fact this tradition has existed from the beginning. He recalls that the Orthodox Church can choose its priests from among married men with exemplary families or from the best celibate men. "So we respect the experience of the Latin Church," the Patriarch comments, "keeping in mind that celibacy only assumes its value in the context of a general asceticism of the monastic type."

On 21 October 1997, Patriarch Bartholomew was in Washington, DC, to receive an honorary doctorate from Georgetown University. In his rather enigmatic address, entitled "Phos Hilaron" ("Joyful Light"),[15] the Patriarch focused on the different paths the Orthodox and Catholic churches have taken, and sought to identify the cause of the divergence. He observed with some pessimism that "the divergence between us continually increases," and that "the end point of our separate courses could turn out to be different." But "our heart is opposed to the specter of an everlasting separation," he said. "Our heart requires that we seek again our common foundations, and the original starting point that we share." Bartholomew said that our problem is not one of personal alienation, jurisdictional arrangements, submission to authority, or the absorption of individuals or groups. "It is something deeper and more substantive," he said. "The manner in which we exist has become ontologically different."

This assertion caused some dismay in the audience, made up largely of Catholic intellectuals. But it is clear that the Patriarch intended to communicate that the way of being of the two churches had become different, making it harder for them to understand one another. He insisted that unless we work toward "one common model of life," it will be impossible to achieve unity. The bulk of his address focused on the Orthodox emphasis on the experiential aspect of the faith, where traditions and dogmas have importance only insofar as they describe an experience of grace. "Therefore the Orthodox Christian does not live in a place of theoretical and conceptual conversations," the Patriarch said, "but rather in a place of an essential and empirical lifestyle and reality as confirmed by grace in the heart. This grace cannot be put in doubt by logic or science or other type of argument."

Bartholomew returned to this theme in a 2004 interview with Gianni Valente in the journal *30 Days*.[16] Here again he downplayed the dogmatic differences between the churches, and focused instead on the divergent spirits that divide them. When asked to comment on the meaning of the excommunications of 1054, the Patriarch said that even if the excommunications had not taken place at that time, such a break was inevitable "because in the West another spirit had infiltrated, different from the one preserved in the East." The root of this division can be found in the "first manifestations of worldly thinking in the Church. True, there were dis-

---

15. Address of His All Holiness Ecumenical Patriarch Bartholomew *Phos Hilarion* ("Joyful Light"). Available online at http://Comcast.net/~t.r.valentine/orthodoxy/texts/Bartholomew_phos.html. Accessed 15 August 2011.

16. Gianni Valente, "The Root of the Schism: Worldly Thinking in the Church," *30 Days*, January 2004.

agreements about specific issues such as the *filioque,* papal primacy, and the celibacy of priests. "Of all these disagreements," the Patriarch said, "the one that can be understood most is why and wherefore the Church of the West founded its hope on worldly power." In fact, the Patriarch asserts that it was this Western tendency to place one's hope in wealth, science, and military power that "prevents an understanding of Orthodox man who . . . sets his hope chiefly in God."

When asked about the evolution of papal authority in the Catholic Church, Bartholomew states unequivocally that the spirit expressed in the words of Christ about coming not to be served but to serve — an attitude that must be assumed also by his apostles — is not found in centralized ecclesiastical power. He said that the idea that Peter had authority over the other apostles is a mistake because Peter was not only the leader of the apostles but also one of them. "The superiority of Peter over the other apostles is put forward to legitimate a primacy of power," in his view. This is why the Orthodox "rightly mistrust all the other papal pretensions, such as infallibility and the new papal dogmas" because they deviate from the ecclesiology of the early church.

Patriarch Bartholomew had expressed similar views about papal primacy in the presence of Pope John Paul II in his homily at a Mass in St. Peter's Basilica for the feast of Sts. Peter and Paul on 29 June 1995.[17] Commenting on Peter's profession of faith as recorded in Matthew 16, he noted that the passage has been studied exhaustively in an attempt to find support for a primacy among the apostles. "Fortunately today," Bartholomew noted, we have learned "to look for a primacy not among persons but rather among the ministries of service." He added that we will be acutely aware of the many ministries of service that stand before us "if we truly are interested not in being 'admired by men' but in being 'pleasing to God.'" Aware that his words might seem offensive to some Catholics, the Patriarch added that in saying these things he did not wish to disturb anyone. "It was, rather, our intent to declare in a solemn way to all of today's Christian world with sincerity and fear of God, our conviction about the necessity of self-criticism and unceasing repentance."[18]

During his tenure Patriarch Bartholomew has also spoken out on

17. "Continuiamo a mirare con timore di Dio alla grazia del calice commune," *L'Osservatore Romano,* 30 June–1 July 1995, 6.

18. See comments by Dimitri Salachas, "Unità: Ricerca irreversibile," *Il regno-attualità,* 14/95, 393-396.

some controversial issues that have arisen. One of these has been the very vocal request by the hierarchy of the Ukrainian Greek Catholic Church that it be raised from its current status of Major Archepiscopal Church to a Patriarchate. The Moscow Patriarchate in particular has always expressed very strong opposition to such a move by the Holy See. In 2003 Cardinal Walter Kasper, then president of the Pontifical Council for Promoting Christian Unity, sent a memorandum on the question to the Moscow Patriarchate that was intended as a basis for conversation. Perhaps misinterpreting the memo as announcing the Holy See's intention to establish a Ukrainian Greek Catholic Patriarchate, the Moscow Patriarchate sent it to the heads of all the other Orthodox churches, requesting their reactions to it. On 17 February 2004, the Moscow Patriarchate issued a press release stating that every single head of the other Orthodox churches had written back stating their strong opposition to a Ukrainian Greek Catholic Patriarchate because they saw it as an unacceptable strengthening or expansion of uniatism on traditionally Orthodox territory. Included was a response from Patriarch Bartholomew who, according to the press release, stated that the establishment of a Ukrainian Greek Catholic Patriarchate would "be regarded as an utterly hostile act against the whole of Orthodoxy."[19]

Patriarch Bartholomew had also written a very strong personal letter directly to Pope John Paul II, dated 29 November, in which he outlined his opposition to a Ukrainian Catholic patriarchate.[20] In it, the Patriarch warns that the position taken in the memo threatened to destroy the progress made in Catholic-Orthodox relations in recent decades, and could bring relations to a new low. The bulk of the letter is an attack on the contents of Cardinal Kasper's memo. He sees it as a reaffirmation of the Catholic policy of uniatism, which is "generally and justifiably considered to be ecclesiologically improper and deceptive, since it aims to entrap members of the Orthodox flock, snatching them away from their Church in order to

19. Press Release, Moscow Patriarchate, 17 February 2004.

20. "Letter patriacale al Papa di Roma Giovanni Paolo II sulla questione concemence l'intenzione del Vaticano di fondare un patriarcato uniate in Ucraina." http://www.ortodossia .it/letteral.htm (Italian translation of the Greek original): "generalmente e giustamente considerate come ecclesiologicamente scorretta e ingannatrice, poichè mira a fagocitare membri del gregge ortodosso strappandoli dalla loro Chiesa per reclutarli in quella Romano-Cattolica. [. . .] È dunque necessario che confermiate, con tutta l'enfasi e convincibilità possibili, al Popolo Ucraino e a tutte le Chiese Ortodosse che non avete intenzione di realizzare la fondazione di un Patriarcato Uniate in Ucraina annunciate dall'Eminentissimo Cardinale Kasper."

absorb them into the Roman Catholic Church." He finds the memo's presentation of the historical development of patriarchates in the Church to be without foundation in the sources, unacceptable, and offensive to the Orthodox. The Patriarch warns that while the establishment of a Ukrainian Greek Catholic Patriarchate would not strengthen uniatism in Ukraine, it would inflame theological polemics on both sides and damage relations between Greek Catholics and Orthodox in that country. A decision would, the Patriarch wrote, provoke a strong reaction from the other Orthodox churches and would probably be a major setback to efforts to continue the theological dialogue between the two churches. It would increase the already growing suspicions among the Orthodox with regard to the Catholic Church and could precipitate a return to the climate of hostility that predominated up until a few decades ago. "Therefore it is necessary that you confirm with the greatest possible emphasis and conviction to the people of Ukraine and to all the Orthodox churches that you do not have the intention to found the Uniate Patriarchate in Ukraine that was announced by His Eminence Cardinal Kasper."

On 3 June 2004, Pope John Paul II received the bishops of the Ukrainian Greek Catholic Church in audience, and spoke about the potential establishment of a patriarchate, which he referred to as "full juridical and ecclesiastical configuration." He expressed the hope that the day might come when he would be able to grant their request. "Meanwhile, as you well know, your request is being seriously studied, also in the light of the evaluations of other Christian Churches."[21] By mid-2011 such a patriarchate had not been established.

One other issue in Orthodox-Catholic relations that should be mentioned here is the decision by Pope Benedict XVI to relinquish the title "Patriarch of the West." There was no official announcement of this decision, but the title was missing in the 2006 edition of the Vatican yearbook, *Annuario Pontificio*. Patriarch Bartholomew did not personally respond to this development, but he presided over a meeting of the Holy Synod of the Ecumenical Patriarchate that issued an official statement on the matter on 8 June 2006.[22] The statement expresses strong regret over this action since

21. "Ukrainian Greek-Catholic Church: Juridical Configuration," *Vatican Information Service,* 3 June 2004.

22. Announcement of the Chief Secretary of the Holy and Sacred Synod regarding the denouncement by Pope Benedict XVI of Rome of the title "Patriarch of the West." Available online at http://www.patriarchate.org/documents/announcement-of-the-denouncement-by-pope-benedict-XVI-of-rome-2006.

this papal title was "the only one that goes back to the period of the Undivided Church of the first millennium, and which has been accepted in the conscience of the Orthodox Church." This was especially disconcerting because the Pope retained other titles which the Orthodox do not accept, including "Vicar of Christ" and "Supreme Pontiff of the Universal Church." At a time when the theological dialogue between the churches was resuming its work and taking up the issue of primacy, "the Ecumenical Patriarchate expresses its wish and prayer that no further difficulties may be added in the discussion of such a thorny problem as that of the primacy of the bishop of Rome."

The Importance of Dialogue

Clearly, Patriarch Bartholomew does not downplay the seriousness of the issues that divide Catholics and Orthodox. But he is also convinced that the best way to overcome these differences is through dialogue. Indeed, it is through conversation and dialogue that various religious groups can come to live together in peace:

> I feel that it is absolutely critical for us to emphasize conversation and to affirm the importance of open, honest dialogue among religions and civilizations as the only way of achieving genuine encounter and communication. Such an interfaith dialogue draws people of diverse religious beliefs and differing cultural backgrounds out of their isolation, preparing them for a process of mutual respect, understanding and acceptance.[23]

As a young boy, Bartholomew recalled seeing Patriarch Athenagoras, a tall man with piercing eyes and a long white beard. In the face of disagreements, Athenagoras was known to call people together to meet, saying to them, "Come, let us look one another in the eyes, and let us then see what we have to say to one another."[24] Bartholomew insists that dialogue is not a denial of religious faith or betrayal of religious affiliation, but a change in attitude, a kind of *metanoia* that signifies seeing things from a different perspective. It is the start of a long and patient process of conversion.

These were the underlying convictions that motivated Patriarch

---

23. Bartholomew, *Encountering the Mystery*, 213.
24. Bartholomew, *Encountering the Mystery*, 215.

Bartholomew in dealing with the crisis the international Catholic-Orthodox dialogue was facing when he took office in 1991. Over the next fifteen years, until the dialogue was able to get back on its feet and resume the theological agenda that had been established at the beginning, the patriarch worked patiently and consistently to move forward.

Tribulation of the Dialogue with Rome

When he became Patriarch, the international dialogue was engaged in the examination of uniatism that had been mandated at the meeting in Freising in 1990. The study resulted in the drafting of an agreed statement for consideration at the seventh plenary of the international dialogue which took place at the Balamand Orthodox School of Theology in Lebanon in June 1993. At Balamand, the dialogue commission adopted a common document entitled, "Uniatism, Method of Union in the Past, and the Present Search for Full Communion."[25] It hinges on two central affirmations: on one hand, "the method which has been called uniatism" is rejected because it is "opposed to the common tradition of our Churches." And on the other hand, it unequivocally affirms that the Eastern Catholic Churches "have the right to exist and to act in response to the spiritual needs of their faithful." It called upon Eastern Catholics to participate in the dialogue at all levels. The document also rules out all forms of proselytism between Catholics and Orthodox, affirming that salvation is available in either church.

Pope John Paul II reacted somewhat cautiously but overall in a positive way to Balamand as an important step forward.[26] In the presence of a Roman delegation to Phanar for the celebration of the feast of St. Andrew in November 1993, the Patriarch spoke about Balamand. He called it an expression of the good intentions of both sides, and continued:

> The joint statement in Balamand through this renewed condemnation of Uniatism as a method of restoring unity certainly bears witness, even if indirectly, to the Western Church's change of heart of such an unacceptable means which was used in the past and for centuries. But also,

25. "Uniatism, Method of Union in the Past, and the Present Search for Full Communion," *Information Service* 83, no. 2 (1993): 96-99.
26. "Visit to Rome of the Delegation of the Ecumenical Patriarchate," *Information Service* 84, nos. 3-4 (1993): 145.

through all that is said about the rights and pastoral needs of the ecclesiastical communities of the Eastern rite issued from Uniatism which are in full communion with the bishop of Rome, it becomes evident that the Orthodox tolerate an ecclesiologically abnormal situation, for the sake of peaceful coexistence of the quarreling parties in the areas of conflict, until the Uniate churches finally understand where they belong.[27]

In contrast to Patriarch Bartholomew's basically positive assessment of Balamand, on the local level reactions were decidedly mixed. In Greece, the Holy Synod of the Orthodox Church condemned the Balamand document in the strongest terms, calling it "utterly foreign to the centuries-long Orthodox tradition, and as antithetical to all the decisions on the dialogue with the Roman Catholic Church taken by the Panorthodox Conferences."[28] In December 1993 the influential monastic community on Mount Athos also sent a letter to Patriarch Bartholomew denouncing Balamand.[29] They objected especially to the document's statement that the Catholic and Orthodox churches both possess the means of salvation. "We are obliged never to accept union," the monks wrote, "or the description of the Roman Catholic Church as a sister church, or the Pope as the canonical bishop of Rome, or the 'church' of Rome as having canonical apostolic succession, priesthood, and mysteries without their expressly stated renunciation of the *filioque,* the infallibility and primacy of the Pope, created grace, and the rest of their cacodoxies." In Romania, the document was approved by the Holy Synod of the Romanian Orthodox Church, but condemned by the country's Catholic bishops. It was only in Ukraine that Balamand gained support from both Eastern Catholics and Orthodox.

In view of the very uneven acceptance of Balamand among the Orthodox churches, Patriarch Bartholomew called the members of the Inter-Orthodox Commission for the Theological Dialogue with the Roman Catholic Church to a meeting at the Ecumenical Patriarchate on 13-14 July 1995. The members agreed that the Balamand document was a step in the

27. "Address of His All Holiness Ecumenical Patriarch Bartholomaios," *Information Service* 85, no. 1 (1994): 38-39.

28. See the Church of Greece's letter to Patriarch Bartholomew, "The Permanent Holy Synod Considers the Balamand Document on Uniatism to Be Unacceptable to the Orthodox" (in Greek), Ἐκκλσιαστικη Ἀλήθια 393, 16 January 1995.

29. "Letter to the Patriarch of Constantinople from the Sacred Community of Mount Athos," *Orthodox Life* 44, no. 4 (1994): 26-29. The Greek original appeared in Ὀρθόδοξος, 18 March 1994.

right direction, and called upon the Catholic Church to avoid, during this delicate period, the celebration of events that evoke negative memories for the Orthodox, such as the 400th anniversary of the Union of Brest (1995-1996), which gave rise to today's Ukrainian Greek Catholic Church. They unanimously proposed that the next theme of the dialogue be "the ecclesiological and pastoral consequences of uniatism."[30]

The patriarch convoked the same commission for another meeting at Phanar on 5-8 December 1997. In his address to the participants, Bartholomew said that "as Orthodox, we must not isolate ourselves and thus miss an occasion the Lord offers us to witness to the truth, to make known with power and conviction our positions which are consistent with the ecumenical councils and the tradition and experience of the holy Fathers of the Orthodox Church." The members examined a draft document entitled "The Canonical and Ecclesiological Consequences of Uniatism" that had been produced by a joint subcommittee of the dialogue in Rome in April 1997. They approved the document as a positive step in the ongoing debates on the question of uniatism.[31]

The Holy See had agreed that uniatism would have to be considered again if the Orthodox were to return to the theological agenda. After many delays, the Joint Coordinating Committee met at Ariccia, near Rome, in June 1998 and continued work on the draft that had been considered by the inter-Orthodox commission in December 1997. The eighth plenary session then took place at Mount St. Mary's College and Seminary in Emmitsburg, Maryland, from 9 to 19 July 2000.

The only text that came out of the Emmitsburg meeting was a Joint Communiqué, issued on 19 July 2000. It notes that the documents previously issued about uniatism had met with strong opposition in some quarters, and that it had been necessary to make another attempt to reach agreement on this "extremely thorny question." The text continued:

> The discussions of this plenary were far reaching, intense and thorough.

---

30. "Réunion au Phanar de la Commission interorthodoxe pour le dialogue avec l'Eglise catholique romaine," *Episkepsis* 521, 31 August 1995, 2-3.

31. "Phanar: Réunion de la Commission interorthodoxe charge du dialogue théologique avec l'Eglise catholique romaine," *Episkepsis* 553, 31 January 1998, 6-7. "En tant qu'Orthodoxes, nous ne devons pas nous isoler et ne pas profiter ainsi de l'occasion que nous offer le Seigneur de témoigner de la vérité, de faire connaître avec force et conviction nos positions conformes aux conciles œcuméniques, à la tradition et à l'expérience des saints Pères de l'Eglise orthodoxe."

They touched upon many theological and canonical questions connected with the existence and the activities of the Eastern Catholic Churches. However, since agreement was not reached on the basic theological concept of unionism, it was decided not to have a common statement at this time. For this reason, the members will report to their Churches who will indicate how to overcome this obstacle for the peaceful continuation of the dialogue.[32]

Clearly an impasse had been reached at Emmitsburg on the question of the status of the Eastern Orthodox churches, and six years would pass before the dialogue would meet again. During the intervening period, great efforts were made to create the conditions under which the dialogue could resume. In a certain sense, this was a re-intensification of the "dialogue of love" that had been forged by Pope John Paul VI and Patriarch Athenagoras, and which had never ceased even after the theological dialogue had begun.

For his part, Ecumenical Patriarch Bartholomew revealed that the situation called for strong leadership, and he began patiently but vigorously to open a path for the future of the dialogue. In the years following the Emmitsburg meeting, the Ecumenical Patriarchate sent out a delegation to visit the various autocephalous Orthodox churches to discuss ways of re-starting the dialogue and to increase the very uneven participation in it by the individual Orthodox churches. In this way the Patriarch was able, mostly behind the scenes, to forge a consensus that the issue of uniatism could not be resolved without first addressing the underlying theological questions, especially relating to primacy in the Church and the Petrine ministry. When Pope John Paul II received a delegation from the Ecumenical Patriarchate in Rome for the feast of Sts. Peter and Paul in 2003, he thanked them for the Ecumenical Patriarchate's "efforts in these past months to coordinate the continuance of the work" of the international dialogue. "I ask you to assure His Holiness of my fervent prayers," the Pope told them, "that this initiative, which is indispensable for our growth in unity, will be crowned with success."[33]

As the atmosphere improved, Patriarch Bartholomew convened an-

---

32. "Joint International Commission for the Theological Dialogue between the Roman Catholic Church and the Orthodox Church, Emmitsburg-Baltimore USA, 9-19 July 2000," *Information Service* 104, no. 3 (2000): 147-148.

33. "Visit to Rome of the Delegation of the Ecumenical Patriarchate, 28-29 June 2003," *Information Service* 113, nos. 2-3 (2003): 61.

other meeting of the Inter-Orthodox Commission of the Theological Dialogue with the Catholic Church at the Ecumenical Patriarchate on 11-13 September 2005. In his speech to the delegates the Patriarch announced that Metropolitan John (Zizioulas) of Pergamon had been appointed the new Orthodox co-chairman of the dialogue to replace Archbishop Sylianos of Australia, who had resigned. He also informed them that as a result of consultations with all the Orthodox churches carried out by the delegation from the Ecumenical Patriarchate, there was now a solid consensus that the dialogue should resume and focus on primacy in the Church. He also expressed the hope that the dialogue would be able to overcome the obstacles that still prevent full communion. He added that while individual churches could have their own opinions on some matters, on matters of faith unity is indispensable and must be restored on the basis of the experience of the undivided church of the first millennium.[34]

The Theological Dialogue Resumed

Everything was now set for the North Plenary Session of the international dialogue, which finally took place in Belgrade from 18 to 25 September 2006, hosted by the Serbian Orthodox Church.[35]

First, the representation of the Orthodox churches was almost complete, demonstrating the effectiveness of the Ecumenical Patriarch's efforts to increase participation. At Emmitsburg, the Orthodox churches of Jerusalem, Serbia, Bulgaria, Georgia, and the Czech and Slovak Republics were not represented, and the churches of Alexandria, Antioch, Russia, Cyprus, Poland, and Finland each sent one representative instead of the allotted two. At the previous meeting in Balamand in 1993, the Orthodox churches of Jerusalem, Serbia, Bulgaria, Georgia, Greece, and the Czech and Slovak Republics were not present, and the churches of Poland, Albania, and Finland sent only one representative.

By contrast, at Belgrade all of the autocephalous and autonomous churches were represented by two members each, except for the churches

---

34. "Réunion au Phanar des members orthodoxes de la commission de dialogue avec L'Eglise catholique romaine," *Episkepsis* 652, 30 September 2005, 5-7. See also the brief report in *Service Orthodoxe de Presse* 301 (September-October 2005): 23-24.

35. "Joint International Commission for the Theological Dialogue between the Roman Catholic Church and the Orthodox Church: Belgrade, Serbia, 18-25 September 2006," *Information Service* 122, no. 2 (2006): 69-71.

of Antioch and Finland, which sent one representative, and the Bulgarian Orthodox delegation, which was not present due to illness. This much more ample representation of the Orthodox churches at Belgrade was a very positive sign.

Second, at Belgrade the dialogue was able to overcome the Emmitsburg impasse, and return to the theological agenda that had been set out in the 1978 plan. It was able, at long last, to consider the text originally prepared sixteen years earlier for the 1990 Freising meeting, and begin to tackle the underlying theological questions that had prevented agreement on the issue of uniatism.

Unfortunately, there was not enough time to finish work on the document in Belgrade, and so the Tenth Plenary was scheduled to take place in one year's time in Ravenna, Italy, from 8 to 14 October 2007.

Orthodox representation at Ravenna was still strong: only the Bulgarians were absent, and also the Russians because of an internal Orthodox dispute. At Ravenna the dialogue was able to finish work on the draft that had been considered in Belgrade. The document was finalized on 13 October and released to the public on 15 November 2007.

The full title of the Ravenna document is "Ecclesiological and Canonical Consequences of the Sacramental Nature of the Church: Ecclesial Communion, Conciliarity, and Authority."[36] Its main purpose is to reflect on how the institutional aspects of the Church visibly express and serve the mystery of *koinonia*. It takes as its starting point the relationship between the one Father and the other two hypostases within the Holy Trinity. It then looks at the relationship of the one and the many at all levels of the Church: local, regional, and universal. In each case, it is a matter of the one primate and the authority he must have in order to ensure unity among the many. This was a challenge both to Catholics, who have tended to downplay the importance of the regional level, and to the Orthodox, who have downplayed the universal level.

Perhaps the most significant section of the document is its treatment of the relationship between the one and the many at the universal level. Its conclusions regarding the primacy of Rome are found in these two paragraphs:

36. *Origins* 37, no. 24 (November 2007): 382-387. For a Catholic evaluation of the Ravenna Document, see Paul McPartlan, "The Ravenna Agreed Statement and Catholic-Orthodox Dialogue," *The Jurist* 69 (2009): 749-765. For an Orthodox perspective, see Kallistos Ware, "The Ravenna Document and the Future of Orthodox-Catholic Dialogue," *The Jurist* 69 (2009): 766-789.

43. Primacy and conciliarity are mutually interdependent. That is why primacy at the different levels of the life of the Church, local, regional and universal, must always be considered in the context of conciliarity, and conciliarity likewise in the context of primacy. Concerning primacy at the different levels, we wish to affirm the following points: 1. Primacy at all levels is a practice firmly grounded in the canonical tradition of the Church. 2. While the fact of primacy at the universal level is accepted by both East and West, there are differences of understanding with regard to the manner in which it is to be exercised, and also with regard to its scriptural and theological foundation.

44. In the history of the East and of the West, at least until the ninth century, a series of prerogatives was recognized, always in the context of conciliarity, according to the conditions of the times, for the *protos* or *kephale* at each of the established ecclesiastical levels: locally, for the bishop as *protos* of his diocese with regard to his presbyters and people; regionally, for the *protos* of each metropolis with regard to the bishops of his province; and for the *protos* of each of the five patriarchates, with regard to the metropolitans of each circumscription; and universally, for the bishop of Rome as *protos* among the patriarchs. This distinction of levels does not diminish the sacramental equality of every bishop or the catholicity of each local Church.

At the conclusion of the Ravenna meeting, it was decided that the next topic would be "The Role of the Bishop of Rome in the Koinonia/Communion of the Church in the First Millennium." The dialogue's coordinating committee met on the island of Crete in the fall of 2008 and produced a draft for consideration at the Eleventh Plenary, which took place in Paphos, Cyprus, in October 2009. The commission was not able to finish work on the text and so scheduled a Twelfth Plenary in Vienna, Austria, which took place from 22 to 27 September 2010.[37]

The Joint Communiqué that was issued at the end of the Vienna session[38] reported that the document on the role of the bishop of Rome in the first millennium was discussed in detail, and found to need further revision. "It was also decided to form a sub-commission to begin consider-

---

37. E. Fortino, "Per cattolici e ortodossi l'appuntamento è a Vienna," *L'Osservatore Romano*, 18 January 2010, 7.

38. "Joint International Commission for Theological Dialogue between the Roman Catholic Church and the Orthodox Church, 12th Plenary Session, Vienna, Austria, 20-27 September 2010," *Information Service* 134, no. 2 (2010): 68-69.

ation of the theological and ecclesiological aspects of Primacy in its relation to Synodality." It appears that the commission has decided that an
analysis of the historical development of the papacy may not be as fruitful
as originally thought, and that the best way forward is to look at the question from a more theological perspective.

Conclusion

The international Catholic-Orthodox dialogue made significant progress
during the first ten years of its existence, but encountered serious difficulties
and an intensification of mistrust and suspicions after the fall of the Communist regimes in Eastern and Central Europe. The fact that it was able to
return to its theological agenda and make new progress after 2006 was due
in no small part to the personal efforts of Ecumenical Patriarch Bartholomew. In the face of strong opposition from some Orthodox quarters, he was
able to forge an Orthodox consensus regarding the continuation of the dialogue and to greatly increase participation by the various churches. Ever the
spokesman for the Orthodox point of view on divisive questions, the Patriarch remains nevertheless an ardent advocate of dialogue as the only path towards greater respect for one another and, in the case of the Catholic
Church, the possibility of the reestablishment of full communion. The patriarch has consistently presented a vision of hope, even at the darkest moments. As he put it so well to Pope John Paul II on 29 June 2004:

> We rejoice to see that you desire and seek this deep ontological unity in
> Christ. This is why we carry on a sincere dialogue with you, Your Holi-
> ness, and with your Church's delegations, and offer you the experience
> concerning the saints of the Orthodox Church, listening with interest to
> all that you explain to us, conversing as brothers with their beloved
> brothers. There are fluctuations in the dialogue because of the difficul-
> ties that have accumulated in the long history of our division. But we are
> confident that it will be brought to a favorable conclusion that is pleas-
> ing to God, and to achieve this we collaborate with you, "looking to Je-
> sus, the pioneer and perfecter of our faith" (Heb. 12:2), without whom
> we can do nothing.[39]

39. Bartholomew, Ecumenical Patriarch of Constantinople, "Dreaming of the Day
When All Obstacles Will Be Removed," *English Weekly L'Osservatore Romano,* 7 July 2004, 5.

There can be no doubt that Patriarch Bartholomew will continue down this hopeful path, doing his utmost to promote unity, in his remaining years at the center of the Orthodox Church.

CHAPTER 6

Orthodox and Reformed in Dialogue:
The Agreed Statement on the Holy Trinity

Joseph D. Small

His All Holiness Ecumenical Patriarch Bartholomew has given personal testimony to his longstanding commitment to ecumenical engagement: "I learned from a tender age to breathe the air of the *oikoumene,* to recognize the breadth of theological discourse, and to embrace the universe of ecclesiastical reconciliation."[1] Bartholomew's witness provides us with a brief summary of his lifetime of dedication to the unity of Christ's church. He breathed it during his studies at the Pontifical Oriental Institute in Rome, the Ecumenical Institute at Bossey, and the University of Munich. He recognized it more clearly during his engagement with the Faith and Order Commission of the World Council of Churches. He embraces it now in his continuing commitment to dialogue with other churches.

The Ecumenical Patriarch's generous Orthodox openness is met by the Reformed Church's abiding commitment to seek and deepen communion with all churches within the one holy catholic and apostolic Church. The stance of the Reformed Church in America is typical: "The Holy Spirit builds one church, united in one Lord and one hope, with one ministry around one table. The Spirit calls all believers in Jesus to respond in worship together, to accept all the gifts from the Spirit, to learn from each other's traditions, to make unity visible on earth."[2] The Reformed tradition

---

1. Bartholomew, Ecumenical Patriarch of Constantinople, *Encountering the Mystery: Understanding Orthodox Christianity Today* (New York: Doubleday, 2008), 14.

2. Reformed Church in America, "Our Song of Hope" (2012). Available online at http://rca.org.

understands that while division among churches obscures the unity of the Church, it does not destroy it, and so the search for *visible* unity among the churches in the one Church is a mandate of the gospel.

Yet it must be acknowledged that at the beginning, and throughout subsequent centuries, circumstances of geography, history, and politics combined to ensure that Reformed and Orthodox churches would remain strangers to one another.

The Fathers and the Reformers

Calvin, Bucer, Zwingli, and their successors gave little attention to the churches of the East. Even as the Reformed movement spread beyond Western Europe, contacts between Orthodox and Reformed were limited by Reformed preoccupation with Rome, and the confinement of most Orthodox churches within the Ottoman Empire. The seventeenth-century episode of Kyrill Loukaris turned mutual unfamiliarity and indifference into detached antagonism which lasted for centuries. Significant contact did not commence until the twentieth century, and sustained theological dialogue between the two traditions is now barely a half-century old.

John Calvin was a child of Western Christendom, an heir to the Great Schism of 1054. Like the other sixteenth-century reformers, his dispute was with Rome; Orthodox Christianity came to his attention primarily in connection with his polemic against practices of the Catholic Church. Calvin's rare mention of Eastern Orthodoxy focused on its use of icons, which he equated with Catholic idolatry. It is worth noting that Reformed "iconoclasm" was not gratuitous aversion to art, but a consequence of deep-seated concern for the true knowledge of God coupled with an acute awareness of the human tendency to construct gods of our own liking. When Calvin wrote that "man's nature, so to speak, is a perpetual factory of idols," he was referring to the human mind's propensity "to imagine a god according to its own capacity."[3] Calvin was convinced that the true knowledge of God comes through proclamation of the word of God and celebration of the sacraments, and that any use of images in the church inevitably distorts God's revelation, leading to worship of a false deity.

Calvin's scant references to Orthodoxy were incidental, therefore, fo-

---

3. John Calvin, *Institutes of the Christian Religion,* ed. John T. McNeill, trans. Ford Lewis Battles (Philadelphia: Westminster Press, 1960) 1.11.8, p. 108.

cused on the perceived similarity between Orthodox icons and the Catholic use of images. "Thus is the foolish scruple of the Greek Christians refuted," claimed Calvin. "For they consider that they have acquitted themselves beautifully if they do not make sculptures of God, while they wantonly indulge in pictures more than any other nation."[4] But even in this florid denunciation of "the Greek Christians," Rome remained Calvin's target. Catholic appeal to the Second Council of Nicaea (A.D. 787) to justify its use of images was met by Calvin's odd rejection of that Council: "For whatever I say, the authority of the Council will occasion a great prejudice in favor of the opposite side. Yet, to speak the truth, this does not move me so much as does the desire to inform my readers how far the madness went of those who were more attached to images than was becoming to Christians."[5]

In his dismissal of Nicaea II, Calvin relied on the *Libri Carolini*, the Frankish church's official declaration that Nicaea II was not a universal council of the church and that its approval of images in the church was invalid. Seemingly unaware that *Libri Carolini* was an element in the ecclesial-political dispute between the Frankish church and the Vatican, Calvin took its account at face value, including its account of the opinions of bishops participating in the Council as well as its rendering of the proofs they employed. This led him to refute the proofs one by one, concluding, "In short, so disgusting are their absurdities that I am ashamed even to mention them."[6] Calvin did not deal with the substance of Nicaea II's conclusion that representational art "is quite in harmony with the history of the spread of the gospel, as it provides confirmation that the becoming man of the Word of God was real and not imaginary, and as it brings us a similar benefit."[7] Instead, he prosecuted his case against Rome by citing earlier traditions, ranging from Lactantius and Eusebius to Augustine and Gregory, all to the effect that images should not be adored or worshiped.

Although Calvin, Zwingli, and Bucer knew little about the Orthodox churches of their time, they were fully familiar with the Greek and Latin Fathers. The Reformation motto *sola scriptura* is often misunderstood to mean that the Tradition of the church has no place in faith's formation and that theology must leap over centuries of Christian existence in direct and

---

4. Calvin, *Institutes* 1.11.4, p. 104.

5. Calvin, *Institutes* 1.11.14, p. 114.

6. Calvin, *Institutes* 1.11.14, p. 115.

7. *Creeds and Confessions of Faith in the Christian Tradition*, vol. 1: *Early, Eastern, and Medieval*, ed. Jaroslav Pelikan and Valerie Hotchkiss (New Haven: Yale University Press, 2003), 217.

exclusive appeal to Scripture. While convinced that Scripture was the ultimate criterion of Christian faith and life, the reformers were also steeped in Renaissance humanism's cry, *ad fontes* — to the sources. They embraced the search for truth in patristic sources and affirmed the Fathers' fidelity to the witness of Scripture.

Ulrich Zwingli does not now enjoy a good reputation, even within Reformed circles, largely because of his memorialist understanding of the Eucharist. Beyond his shallow view of the Lord's Supper, however, he was a subtle theologian who was familiar with the deep Tradition of the church. He owned and annotated works of the Greek and Latin Fathers: Ambrose, Augustine, Athanasius, Basil of Caesarea, John Chrysostom, Cyprian, Cyril of Alexandria, John of Damascus, Gregory the Great, Gregory of Nazianzus, Gregory of Nyssa, Hilary of Poitiers, Irenaeus of Lyon, Jerome, Lactantius, Origen, and Tertullian, as well as standard medieval collections of excerpts from the Fathers.[8] Irena Backus characterizes Zwingli's engagement with the Fathers as "a tacit hierarchy of sacred texts . . . with the Bible at the top broadening out to a pyramid of patristic evidence, indispensable in its turn for construction of a biblical theology."[9] The same assessment can be applied to Bucer and Calvin.

Calvin followed Zwingli and Bucer in broad knowledge of patristic sources, using them in both polemical and constructive ways. His humanistic education at the universities of Paris, Orléans, and Bourges immersed him in classical antiquity, "pagan" as well as Christian (Calvin's first published work was a commentary on Seneca's *De Clementia*). There is no doubt that he read widely in the Fathers and that they were an important, albeit subsidiary, source for his biblical and theological work.

While a young man, at the very beginning of his first stay in Geneva, Calvin participated in the Lausanne Disputation between Swiss reformers and Catholics. His participation in the disputation was limited. Because he was subordinate to the older and more experienced Farel and Viret, he listened throughout the debates, speaking only twice. His only substantive intervention was occasioned by the Catholic charge that the reformers dishonored "the holy doctors of antiquity." He responded spontaneously that if the charge were true, "we should not at all refuse to be judged by the whole world as not only audacious but beyond measure arrogant." He then

---

8. Irena Backus, "Ulrich Zwingli, Martin Bucer, and the Church Fathers," in *The Reception of the Church Fathers in the West,* ed. Irena Backus (Leiden: E. J. Brill, 1997), vol. 1, 628ff.

9. Backus, "Ulrich Zwingli, Martin Bucer, and the Church Fathers," vol. 1, 644.

turned the tables on the Catholic disputants, saying of the reformers, "we take the trouble to read them and use the help of their teaching."[10] He then proceeded to demonstrate his claim by extensively quoting patristic texts from memory.

The pervasive Catholic charge of Reformation departure from the faith of the early church may account for Calvin's steady use of patristic sources as evidence in his disputes with Catholic teaching. As early as the Prefatory Address to King Francis in the first edition of the *Institutes of the Christian Religion* (1536) Calvin took note of the Catholic charge that the reformers were out of accord with the deep Tradition of the church, promoting instead a novel form of Christian faith. "They unjustly set the ancient fathers against us (I mean the ancient writers of a better age of the church)," wrote Calvin. "If the contest were to be determined by patristic authority the tide of victory — to put it very modestly — would turn to our side." He went on to insist that "we do not despise [the Fathers]; in fact, if it were to our present purpose I could with no trouble at all prove that the greater part of what we are saying today meets their approval."[11] This defense of the reformers' fidelity to the Fathers was included in every edition of the *Institutes,* both Latin and French, from the first to the final revision in 1560.

As Calvin refined the *Institutes,* wrote theological treatises, and composed commentaries on Scripture, he continued to demonstrate that reformation theology met with the approval of the Fathers. Although Augustine was cited more than any other, Calvin often referred to the Fathers of the first three centuries — Justin, Irenaeus, Tertullian, Cyprian, and Origen; and the Fathers of the fourth and fifth centuries — Athanasius, Chrysostom, Cyril of Alexandria, Epiphanius, and the Cappadocians, as well as Hilary, Ambrose, Augustine, and Jerome. While his references were often selective, for his purpose was to enlist the Fathers as allies in Reformation contention with Rome, they demonstrate Calvin's grasp of patristic sources.

Calvin's use of the Fathers went beyond polemic, however; his references to the patristic era also served constructive purposes. In the *Institutes'* chapter on the Trinity, Calvin referred extensively to the Arian controversy and its resolution at the Council of Nicaea. He was pointedly grateful for

10. "Two Discourses on the Articles," in *Calvin: Theological Treatises,* ed. J. K. S. Reid (Philadelphia: Westminster Press, 1954), 38.

11. Calvin, *Institutes,* "Prefatory Address to King Francis I of France," p. 18.

patristic teaching on the Trinity, both before and after Nicaea. Notably, he quoted with enthusiasm Gregory Nazianzus — "I cannot think on the one without quickly being enriched by the splendor of the three; nor can I discern the three without being straightway carried back to the one" — commenting that Gregory's saying "vastly delights me."[12] Calvin's approval of the patristic era went beyond references to particular Church Fathers, for he stressed his "embrace and reverence as holy the early councils, such as those of Nicaea, Constantinople, Ephesus I, Chalcedon, and the like . . . For they contain nothing but the pure and genuine exposition of Scripture, which the holy fathers applied with spiritual prudence . . ."[13]

Ecumenical Patriarch Bartholomew has noted that "the authority of the Fathers depends less on antiquity; it is not related to their *historical* proximity to the early Church and Christ . . . Their authority is grounded, rather, on the quality of their testimony; it is related to their closeness to the *faith* — and not simply to the times — of the Apostles."[14] Calvin would surely agree, for the faith of the apostles made known through Scripture is the standard by which to judge all subsequent theological exposition. It is their fidelity to the apostolic witness in Scripture that commends the Fathers, just as it is the standard by which all subsequent theology and practice is judged. That is why Calvin rejected the views of some who were closer to the earliest church such as Marcion and Sabellius, while approving of Irenaeus and Athanasius. Calvin, like Bartholomew, "looks for consistency with Scripture and tradition."[15]

While Calvin's knowledge of the Fathers was broad and deep, it was wholly divorced from knowledge of or relationship with the sixteenth-century Orthodox Church. In the years that followed Calvin and other early reformers, Reformed-Orthodox interactions were characterized by benign indifference, interrupted only by the unfortunate dynamics surrounding Kyrill Loukaris, Ecumenical Patriarch of Constantinople from 1620 to 1638. Kyrill became aware of Reformed theology during studies in Italy and a brief assignment in Poland. During his time as Patriarch of Alexandria he read extensively in Calvin's *Institutes,* motivated in part by his appreciation of the ways that Reformation critique contributed to Orthodoxy's intensifying conflict with Rome. Through acquaintance with Cal-

---

12. Calvin, *Institutes* 1.13.17, p. 141.
13. Calvin, *Institutes* 4.9.8, pp. 1171-1172.
14. Bartholomew, *Encountering the Mystery*, 39.
15. Bartholomew, *Encountering the Mystery*, 9.

vin's writings and by means of emissaries who met with Reformed theologians in Switzerland, England, and Holland, Kyrill became convinced that Reformation doctrine was fully compatible with Orthodox faith, and that, moreover, it bolstered his commitment to ongoing reform of the church.

Following his election as Ecumenical Patriarch in 1620, Kyrill continued to develop a Reformed theological approach within the Orthodox tradition. In 1629, he summed up his convictions in a formal confession, which was first published in Geneva in Latin, and only later in Greek. Not surprisingly, Kyrill's confession was unwelcome in Orthodox churches, and it strengthened his opponents in ecclesial, political, and diplomatic circles. Theological opposition within the Orthodox Church and diplomatic opposition by European powers combined to bring about Kyrill's downfall. He was accused of treason by the Ottoman sultan and executed in 1638.

The details of the Kyrill Loukaris affair are less important than its destructive effect on Orthodox-Reformed relations, alienation that lasted for centuries thereafter. Soon after Kyrill's death, a Synod met in Constantinople to condemn him and his teachings. The Synod declared that "Kyrill, called Loukaris, who through the Articles of his confession brought the whole Eastern church into disrepute as being favorably disposed to Calvinism, is anathematized."[16] This was followed by further condemnations of Kyrill's confession at the Synods of Iasi and Jerusalem. For their part, European Reformed theologians, who had romanticized Kyrill's views during his lifetime, saw his condemnation as evidence of the Eastern Church's dogmatic provincialism. In Reformed hands, Kyrill's confession was soon reduced to a mere weapon in anti-Catholic polemics. Whatever the reality of Kyrill Loukaris, the result was Orthodox hostility to "Calvinism" and Reformed disparagement of Orthodoxy.

And yet, while Orthodox and Reformed churches remained distantly hostile, Calvin's high regard for the Fathers and the (first four) ecumenical councils carried into seventeenth-century Reformed scholasticism and beyond. Patristic scholarship deepened and Reformed theology continued to draw on the Fathers, particularly with regard to the doctrine of the Trinity. The continuing legacy of Reformed regard for the Fathers and the Ecumenical Councils kept alive an inheritance shared with Orthodoxy, even when ecclesial relations were virtually nonexistent. Thus it was not coincidental

16. Cited in Lukas Vischer, "The Legacy of Kyrill Loukaris: A Contribution to the Orthodox-Reformed Dialogue," *Mid-Stream* 25 (April 1986): 175.

that it was a Reformed theologian and patristics scholar who initiated twentieth-century Reformed engagement with the Orthodox churches.

From Consultation to Dialogue

Orthodox participation in the 1910 Edinburgh Missionary Conference, and in Faith and Order conferences in Lausanne (1927) and Edinburgh (1937), initiated modest contact between Orthodox and Reformed representatives. However, it was not until the establishment of the World Council of Churches that tentative conversations began, not only in WCC forums, but also locally in Romania and other Eastern European countries. Yet these encounters remained informal and episodic. It was the mid-1970s initiative of Scottish theologian Thomas F. Torrance that led to formal consultations between the World Alliance of Reformed Churches and the Ecumenical Patriarchate.

T. F. Torrance, long-tenured professor of Christian dogmatics at New College, Edinburgh, was a theologian with wide-ranging intellectual interests, leading to publications of lasting influence in historical, ecumenical, and constructive theology.[17] His early commitment to the abiding relevance of the early Fathers was confirmed and deepened by his studies in Basel during 1937 and 1938, where he was profoundly influenced by Karl Barth. Torrance's studies were interrupted by World War II military service, but he was awarded a Basel doctorate in 1946 upon approval of his thesis, "The Doctrine of Grace in the Apostolic Fathers." Torrance's lifelong work in patristics led to numerous journal articles and books such as *The Incarnation: Ecumenical Studies in the Nicene-Constantinopolitan Creed; The Trinitarian Faith: The Evangelical Theology of the Ancient Catholic Church;* and *Divine Meaning: Studies in Patristic Hermeneutics.* His commitment to ecumenical theology is seen in *Conflict and Agreement in the Church* (2 vols.); *Theology in Reconciliation: Essays toward Evangelical and Catholic Unity in East and West;* and *Trinitarian Perspectives: Toward Doctrinal Agreement.* Torrance's patristic studies and ecumenical commitments combined to shape his expanding engagement with the contemporary Orthodox Church, expressed in both scholarly and popular contexts.

Torrance's historical, theological, and ecumenical interests led to his

---

17. Torrance's bibliography in Alister McGrath's *T. F. Torrance: An Intellectual Biography* (London: T&T Clark, 1999) covers forty-seven pages.

key role in the genesis of theological consultations between Reformed churches and the Orthodox Church. Informal, local conversations had begun to occur episodically in Eastern Europe following the Fourth World Conference on Faith and Order (1963), but formal, ongoing contact at the international level was nonexistent. Nevertheless, local contacts helped to overcome wariness in both Orthodox and Reformed churches, preparing the way for a proposal for a more intentional relationship. Even so, it was not until 1977 that Torrance made the first move. "It seemed to me," he wrote, "that an attempt should be made to engage in formal theological consultations with the Ecumenical Patriarchate with a view to clarifying together the classical bases of Orthodox and of Reformed theology, and in the hope of reaching the same kind of profound accord with respect to the 'theological axis' of Athanasian/Cyriline theology, to which the Reformed Church has looked as having regulative force in its understanding of Christian faith hardly less than the Greek Orthodox Church."[18]

The appropriate Reformed partner in Torrance's proposed "consultations" was the World Alliance of Reformed Churches, a loose association of several hundred Reformed churches scattered throughout the world. Although the bonds uniting the Reformed churches were weak, WARC's Department of Theology was actively committed to ecumenical dialogue that would have a bearing on relationships that could lead to a dialogue. These conversations led to Lochman's formal letter on behalf of WARC to His All Holiness Dimitrios I, proposing a series of consultations between the Ecumenical Patriarchate and the World Alliance of Reformed Churches. The Ecumenical Patriarch's positive response led Torrance to develop a proposal that was eventually adopted in slightly revised form — the "Agreed Understanding of the Theological Development and Eventual Direction of Orthodox/Reformed Conversations Leading to Dialogue."

Torrance's outline for the future of "Orthodox/Reformed Conversations" was both cautious and bold. Because substantive contact between Orthodox and Reformed had been virtually nonexistent, formal dialogue was premature. The more circumspect "conversation" and "consultation" provided a free space for both Orthodox and Reformed to explore possibilities without committing themselves to the constraints of a formal ecclesial dialogue. Yet Torrance was also bold, for he proposed that the series of consultations focus on the doctrine of the Trinity. Torrance believed

18. T. F. Torrance, *Theological Dialogue between Orthodox and Reformed Churches*, vol. 1 (Edinburgh: Scottish Academic Press, 1985), x.

that for both WARC and the Ecumenical Patriarchate, mutual understanding of Trinity was the essential prerequisite for the viability of future consultations on other themes. Ecumenical dialogues often assume agreement on foundational theological matters, focusing instead on neuralgic issues that divide churches. The Orthodox/Reformed conversation focused on the crucial issue that could initiate a relationship based on foundational agreement. Only from acknowledgment of shared Trinitarian faith, Torrance believed, could the two church bodies proceed to discuss the nature of the church, ministry, and sacraments.

Istanbul 1979

The first consultation took place in Istanbul in 1979, followed by Geneva in 1981, and Chambésy in 1983. At the initial meeting, Torrance presented a paper, "Memoranda on Orthodox/Reformed Relations," that began by stating, "The Reformed Church knows the Greek Orthodox Church for its faithfulness to Apostolic Faith and Practice, and to the Catholic theology of the Greek Fathers to which the whole Church of Christ in East and West is so deeply indebted."[19] He went on to acknowledge that during the long separation of East from West, Orthodox churches had developed liturgical patterns and forms of piety that seem strange to Reformed Churches, just as Reformed practices seem strange to the Orthodox. Yet, "Reformed churches do not regard these differences in forms of piety as entering into the substance of the faith, or as ruling out genuine koinonia between them and the Orthodox Churches."[20] With a genuine expression of appreciation and an honest acknowledgment of difference behind him, Torrance then dove into a Reformed exposition of Trinity and apostolic faith. Metropolitan Emilianos Timiadis responded in kind with his paper, "God's Immutability and Communicability." These two papers provided the basis for extensive discussion that laid the groundwork for continued consultations.

Geneva 1981

While the first consultation explored areas of substantial theological coherence, it became clear that the relative authority of the conversation partners

19. Torrance, *Theological Dialogue*, vol. 1, 5.
20. Torrance, *Theological Dialogue*, vol. 1, 5.

presented difficulties that had to be addressed. At the 1981 Geneva meeting, Chrysostomos Konstantinidis put the matter bluntly: "As for the Reformed world, and the Churches issuing from the Reformation, it is well known that from the Orthodox point of view the question of authority in the Church is not only considered as an absolutely critical point of dialogue, but it also stands out as a condition of entering into theological dialogue with them."[21] The question posed to the Reformed delegation was twofold. First, how can there be authority and oversight *(episcopé)* in a church that is not episcopally ordered, and second, what authority did the World Alliance of Reformed Churches have vis-à-vis its member churches in order to secure their binding acceptance of ecumenical consensus statements?

Both questions are familiar to Reformed churches. They continue to be asked by various dialogue partners, and they continue to be asked by the Reformed churches themselves. They are not confined to the Reformed world, however. The problem of authority in its (post-)modern form is a reality in all churches, whether episcopally, synodically, or congregationally ordered. The authority of world confessional organizations is an issue that WARC did not resolve by changing its name to the "World *Communion* of Reformed Churches." The Orthodox question is not merely an organizational one, for it goes to the heart of what koinonia actually means within traditions and among churches.

Hans-Helmut Esser provided a Reformed response to the Orthodox questions in his paper "The Authority of the Church and Authority in the Church according to the Reformed Tradition." Noting that Reformed ecclesiology derives from Christology, Esser stated that

> in ecclesiology, therefore, [the Reformed doctrine] seeks to do justice to the Chalcedonian formula; in other words, in the interests of the authority of Christ himself, to clear the area which lies between the monophysite error on the one side and the dyophysite on the other. In other words, no triumphalist identification of the Church's authority with the Divinity of Christ, but also no skeptical *a priori* divorce between the lowliness of the Church and the promise of the presence of its risen Lord.[22]

Esser went on to outline the nature of synodical authority in the Reformed tradition. First, proposals that affect Christian faith and life must

---

21. Torrance, *Theological Dialogue*, vol. 1, 74.
22. Torrance, *Theological Dialogue*, vol. 1, 50.

be oriented to Scripture, in continuity with the confession of past generations, and faithful to the call of the Triune God in the contemporary situation. Discussion of proposals must be articulated unambiguously in language that is intelligible to the whole church. Second, there should be
maximum unanimity in decisions regarding important matters. Third,
when decisions about doctrine and life are not unanimous, the voting results and the views of the minority must be made public. These three criteria, Esser said, enable church members to make spiritual appraisal of synodical decisions.

Chambésy 1983

Clearly, divergent Orthodox and Reformed understandings of ecclesial authority were not reconciled at the Geneva consultation, nor have they been
since. Nonetheless, mutual understanding was sufficient to proceed to the
1983 consultation at Chambésy, where questions of church and authority
were placed within an explicitly Trinitarian framework. Torrance's paper,
"The Trinitarian Foundation and Character of Faith and of Authority in
the Church," began by presupposing the Orthodox (and orthodox) doctrine of the Holy Trinity. He stressed that, in line with Athanasius and
Gregory Nazianzus, the theological terms used — *ousia, hypostasis, pēgē,
archē, aitia* — are stretched beyond their ordinary sense when applied to
God. "This means that we must take care that the natural images and anal-
ogies which this human language carries are not read back into God but
are critically controlled by the self-revelation of God which they are employed to articulate."[23]

In characteristic Reformed fashion, Torrance insisted that theological
language must be governed by revelation. We can know the God who sur-
passes all created being only because he has made himself accessible to us
in Jesus Christ under the conditions of human existence in a way that is
completely faithful to who God is in himself. Torrance made clear the
Trinitarian basis of the human possibility of the knowledge of God:
"Through the incarnate Son and in the mission of the Spirit a way has been
opened up for us to the Father, so that we may know God in some real
measure as he is in himself."[24]

23. Torrance, *Theological Dialogue*, vol. 1, 79.
24. Torrance, *Theological Dialogue*, vol. 1, 80.

Torrance then carried Trinitarian epistemology into his discussion of authority in the church. Trinitarian language shapes all theological language so that Christ's *alētheia* and *exousia* must be seen as one in the *ego eimi* of his being. Since authority and truth are one in Christ, so must they be in the church. "Just as Irenaeus operated with a concept of embodied truth and embodied doctrine in the Church," Torrance said, "so he operated also with a concept of *embodied authority,* with a ministry with which Christ shared *exousia* in its proclamation of the gospel, and pastoral care of the people to be exercised according to the *hypodeigma* of service exhibited by Christ himself, but with the promise that he himself would be with the ministry so that the proclamation and teaching of the Word of the Gospel in his name would indeed be empowered by the saving Word of God."[25] Since truth and authority are one in Christ, embodied authority is not exercised in judicial relations, but only through union and communion with Christ, "which means that authority in the church is actualized and exercised in Christ only by way of *koinōnia.*"[26]

Metropolitan Emianos Timiadis also addressed "The Trinitarian Structure of the Church and Its Authority." His approach, while not in contradiction to Torrance's, displayed differences between Orthodox and Reformed attitudes toward theological expression. In typical Reformed fashion, Torrance set forth a logical progression from history through epistemology, doctrine, and ecclesiology to authority. Timiadis, on the other hand, focused on the lived faith and faithfulness of the church, seen most clearly in the Eucharist. The church is a divine-human reality, he wrote, for "in it the believers are members of the one Body of Christ . . . The believers participate in the fullness of the life of Christ, experienced by receiving his body and blood."[27]

In a moving section of his paper, Timiadis asked,

How, despite so many attacks by pagans, by heretics one after the other, by unworthy bishops who even surrendered to heretical bodies, did the Church remain true, one, and apostolic? The answer is found in the fact that, in spite of radical changes and upheavals, she was protected and guided in all the vicissitudes of history by the blessed Trinity. Thus, remaining faithful to her commission, the Church did not abuse this priv-

---

25. Torrance, *Theological Dialogue,* vol. 1, 116.
26. Torrance, *Theological Dialogue,* vol. 1, 116.
27. Torrance, *Theological Dialogue,* vol. 1, 123-124.

ilege, by adding anything new or removing elements of the apostolic *didaskalia*. In this fact lies her authority.[28]

It is important to see that both Timiadis and Torrance ground authority in truth, and ground truth in Christ, so that truth and authority are one. Reformed and Orthodox distinctives are displayed in the different ways that Timiadis and Torrance articulated shared convictions. It was the recognition of shared convictions that enabled the Orthodox and Reformed partners to conclude their consultations with a firm decision to commence a formal, ongoing dialogue. The concluding affirmation of the consultation series noted that "Deep soundings were taken on both sides to see if there were sufficient common ground regarding the canon of truth, the nature and place of authority in the Church, as well as the Trinitarian foundation and character of the Faith."[29] These deep soundings discovered common ground, and so the Orthodox and Reformed Churches reached an important new stage in their relationship.

From Dialogue to Agreed Statement on the Holy Trinity

The official Orthodox-Reformed International Dialogue was launched at a 1986 planning meeting in Chambésy. It was agreed that the dialogue theme would be "The Doctrine of the Holy Trinity on the Basis of the Niceno-Constantinopolitan Creed," and that sessions of the dialogue would meet at Leuenberg in 1988 and Minsk in 1990. Remarkably, these two dialogue meetings were sufficient to produce the "Agreed Statement on the Holy Trinity." Major credit for this extraordinary achievement must go to Prof. Torrance of the World Alliance of Reformed Churches and Protopresbyter Dr. George Dion Dragas of the Ecumenical Patriarchate; they prepared the preliminary draft that was discussed, refined, and then approved at the second dialogue session.

Leuenberg 1988

Although the dialogue assumed the results of previous consultations, the presence of new delegates necessitated questions about historical and

---

28. Torrance, *Theological Dialogue*, vol. 1, 152-153.
29. Torrance, *Theological Dialogue*, vol. 1, 158.

ecclesiological matters. Discussion of the Orthodox understanding of "the undivided Church" and the Reformed principle of *ecclesia reformata semper reformanda* led to even more questions, but both delegations agreed that these matters should be deferred until "a later stage, after the theme of the Holy Trinity as the source of faith, worship, and life of the church was adequately discussed and clear conclusions drawn."[30] Before preparatory papers were read and discussed, the Reformed delegation made an important declaration: "As regards the *filioque* clause, the Reformed members stated the prevailing opinion among the Reformed Churches, according to which the above clause should be removed from use since it did not belong to the original version, but that the theological issues related to the *filioque* controversy should be discussed with a view to reaching a common mind."[31]

Four papers were read, two from each side — Torrance: "The Triunity of God in the Nicene Theology of the Fourth Century"; Dragas: "St. Athanasius on the Holy Spirit and the Trinity"; Tityu Koev: "The Doctrine of the Holy Trinity on the Basis of the Nicene-Constantinopolitan Symbol of Faith"; and Lukas Vischer, "The Holy Spirit — Source of Sanctification: Reflections on Basil the Great's Treatise on the Holy Spirit." These scholarly, even dense presentations were necessary elements in shaping the emerging conviction that the Orthodox and Reformed Churches were in broad agreement on the essential elements of the doctrine of the Trinity.

Broad agreement did not mean that Reformed and Orthodox articulations were identical in all respects, however. While the papers of Torrance and Dragas cohered in approach and substance, a clear difference in tone was evident in the papers of Koev and Vischer. While both affirmed the absolute centrality of the Trinity, there was a marked disparity in the character of their deference to the Nicene Creed. Koev concluded his exposition of Nicene teaching with a sweeping declaration that "the significance of the dogma of the Holy Trinity . . . is all-embracing and serves the correct formation of the Christian view of life. . . . The dogma of the Holy Trinity is the source of our confidence. It is the solid basis of our hope for salvation."[32] Vischer, on the other hand, concluded his paper by noting, "One of the characteristics of the Reformed churches is that they never regard the Church's confession of faith as finally closed." His soft acknowledgment

---

30. T. F. Torrance, *Theological Dialogue between Orthodox and Reformed Churches*, vol. 2 (Edinburgh: Scottish Academic Press, 1993), xii.

31. Torrance, *Theological Dialogue*, vol. 2, xii.

32. Torrance, *Theological Dialogue*, vol. 2, 82-83.

that "the ancient church creeds in particular still are signposts and guides even for the present time" would not have been voiced by Koev or Dragas (or by Torrance!).[33]

The dialogue session addressed important questions such as the character of patristic teaching and its relation to the Tradition and faith of the church, the relation of Scripture to the Creed, and the relationship between Trinitarian dogma and experience. Predictably, Orthodox and Reformed articulations were not identical, yet at the conclusion of the meeting there was sufficient coherence on the central question of the doctrine of the Trinity, that Dragas and Torrance were asked to draft a "Working Document on the Holy Trinity" to be offered at the next meeting of the dialogue. The explicit hope of both Orthodox and Reformed was that the "Working Document" would provide an acceptable basis for formal theological agreement.

Minsk 1990

As in the Leuenberg session of the dialogue, four significant papers were presented: both Christos Voulgaris and Christopher Kaiser addressed "The Biblical and Patristic Doctrine of the Trinity," while Bruce Rigdon and Archbishop Simon of Ryazan and Kasimov dealt with the Trinity and worship. But it was the "Working Paper on the Holy Trinity" that was the central object of discussion. The preparatory papers at both Leuenberg and Minsk played an important part, however, for the eight carefully articulated expressions of Reformed and Orthodox views on the doctrine of the Trinity demonstrated sufficient agreement to proceed with a common statement. As Torrance recalled, "Both the Orthodox and the Reformed readily acknowledged that they have different emphases in their approaches to the Doctrine of the Holy Trinity, but they insisted that they agree on the content of the doctrine."[34]

Unfortunately, Fr. Dr. Dragas was unable to be present, so Torrance presented the working paper that he and Dragas had prepared. At the outset, he recalled the bold purpose of the dialogue:

It was to penetrate as deeply as possible into the one Apostolic foundation of the Faith, God's unique revelation of himself through himself as

---

33. Torrance, *Theological Dialogue*, vol. 2, 104.
34. Torrance, *Theological Dialogue*, vol. 2, xxi.

Father, Son and Holy Spirit, upon which the whole Church rests, in order to cut beneath and behind doctrinal differences that have arisen between Eastern and Western, Catholic and Evangelical traditions, in the hope of reaching a fundamental agreement on the Doctrine of the Trinity on the basis of which we might then reach authentic concord in other areas of belief as well. We had particularly in mind Christology and Soteriology, and the doctrines of the Eucharist and the Church as the body of Christ, all of which have a deep Trinitarian basis.[35]

The working paper was intended to provide the basis for fulfilling the hope of the dialogue, and it accomplished its purpose. Careful, sustained attention to the text led to revisions, primarily for the sake of clarity. The revised document was accepted as the conjoint "Agreed Statement on the Holy Trinity." A joint statement issued at the conclusion of the Minsk session concluded by stating, "We affirm that faith in the Holy Trinity is the basis of our worship, prayers and praise, and provides the perspective for our witness in the world. It is incumbent on the Churches to communicate this Trinitarian faith in all their life and activities."[36]

Although agreement had been reached, it was recognized that the text had to be "tidied up" before final, formal approval at the concluding session of the dialogue, to be held at Kappel, near Zurich, in 1992. In addition, the Reformed delegation suggested that a brief document underlining significant features of the Agreed Statement might be useful in interpreting it more broadly. The Orthodox delegation agreed. Torrance and Dragas were asked to prepare a draft to be reviewed by a small joint working group meeting at Chambésy the following year. The working group suggested clarifications and revisions, recommending that "Significant Features: A Common Reflection on the Agreed Statement" be presented for approval, as an interpretive supplement to the "tidied-up" text of the Agreed Statement. Both the Agreed Statement and the Common Reflection were formally adopted at Kappel in March, 1992.

Agreed Statement on the Holy Trinity

The Agreed Statement is precisely that, a statement that speaks with one voice. Unlike many reports that emerge from ecumenical dialogues, the

35. Torrance, *Theological Dialogue*, vol. 2, 115-116.
36. Torrance, *Theological Dialogue*, vol. 2, xxiii.

Agreed Statement does not set out differing emphases or divergent positions. It begins by stating that "We confess together the evangelical and ancient Faith of the Catholic Church . . . and it is common confession that is articulated throughout."[37] The Agreed Statement is divided into eight brief, densely packed sections, each one of which contains affirmations that are of enduring importance.

The Self-Revelation of God as Father, Son, and Holy Spirit

The opening section emphasizes that the doctrine of the Trinity is not a theological construction imposed upon Scripture. Rather, "According to the Holy Gospel God has revealed himself in the Father, the Son, and the Holy Spirit, as *'through the Son who have access to the Father in one Spirit'* (Eph. 2.18)." Further texts are cited to stress that Scripture is "the foundation of the Apostolic doctrine of the Trinity in Unity and the Unity in Trinity: one Being, three Persons." The section concludes with a significant theme that pervades the whole. Echoing the words of Gregory Nazianzus that so delighted Calvin, the Agreed Statement declares that "To believe in the Unity of God apart from the Trinity is to limit the truth of divine Revelation. It is through the divine Trinity that we believe in the divine Unity, and through the divine Unity that we believe in the divine Trinity." This formulation is intended to overcome the common, yet mistaken, view that Latin theology moves from the Oneness of God to the three Persons, while Greek theology moves from the three Persons to the Oneness of God.

Three Divine Persons

Contrary to some current sensibilities, the Agreed Statement affirms that "In the New Testament witness to God's Revelation *'the Father,' 'the Son,'* and *'the Holy Spirit'* are unique and proper names denoting three distinct Persons or real Hypostases which are neither exchangeable nor interchangeable while nevertheless of one and the same divine Being." The sec-

---

37. Jeffrey Gros, Harding Meyer, and William G. Rusch, eds., *Growth in Agreement II* (Geneva: WCC Publications, 2000), 280. This and all subsequent quotations from the Agreed Statement are taken from the text of the "Agreed Statement on the Holy Trinity" on pages 280-284 of *Growth in Agreement II*.

tion proceeds with careful affirmations of both the distinction of the Persons and their consubtantiality.

Whereas the opening section appealed to Scripture as warrant, this section, as well as subsequent sections, elucidates affirmations by reference to the Fathers. Thus, in discussing the three hypostases, the Agreed Statement cites Gregory the Theologian: "One is not more or less God, nor is One before and after Another . . . for there is no greater or less in respect of the Being or the consubstantial Persons." At the heart of this often technical section lies the crucial declaration that "the Holy Trinity is thus perfectly homogeneous and unitary, both in the threeness and oneness of God's activity, and in the threeness and oneness of his own eternal unchangeable Being." Who God is toward us he is in himself, and who God is in himself he is toward us.

Eternal Relations in God

Consistent with the initial agreement that the proper form of the Creed does not include the *filioque,* the Agreed Statement affirms that "the Son is eternally begotten of the Father and the Spirit eternally proceeds from the Father and abides in the Son." This formulation honors both the Orthodox concern for the integrity of the Creed and the Reformed concern that the Holy Spirit not be understood apart from the Son. The conjoining of the three Persons through their special relations is matched by their conjoining in "all the manifestations of God's activity, in creation, providence, revelation, and salvation, as they are consummated in the Incarnate activity of the Son." Again, this contrasts with some current formulations that divide the Trinity into discrete activities, such as the replacement of "Father, Son, and Holy Spirit" by "Creator, Redeemer, and Sustainer."

The Order of Divine Persons in the Trinity

The Trinitarian references in the New Testament vary in the order in which they mention Father, Son, and Holy Spirit, thereby indicating that "the order does not detract from full equality between the three Divine Persons." Nevertheless, the Agreed Statement recognizes in the institution of baptism a "significant coordination which places the Father first, the Son second, and the Spirit third." This is not to be understood as an order of descending rank, however, but the order inherent in "the fact that the Son is begotten of the Father and the Spirit proceeds from the Father." Again, this is not only a statement about eternal relations in God, for "this applies also to the unique revelation of the Father through the Incarnation of his only begotten Son and the sending of the Holy Spirit by the Father in the name of the Son."

Trinity in Unity and Unity in Trinity; the One Monarchy

Orthodox references to the Monarchy of the Father are often misunderstood to imply superiority, the Father's "rule" over the Son and Spirit. Therefore, the Agreed Statement draws heavily upon patristic sources to emphasize that "since there is only one Trinity in Unity, and one Unity in Trinity, there is only one indivisible Godhead, and only one *Arche* (αρχή) or *Monarchia* (μοναρχία)." No fewer than four patristic sources are cited to emphasize that the Monarchy is inseparable from the Trinity, but not limited to one person. The *Monarchia* of the Father is only and perfectly what it is in the Father's relation to the Son and the Spirit within the one indivisible Being of God. As such, then, "the Monarchy of the Father within the Trinity is not exclusive of the Monarchy of the whole undivided Trinity in relation to the whole of creation."

The Perichoresis or Mutual Indwelling of Father, Son, and Holy Spirit

Agreement concerning eternal relations in God is carried further with the affirmation that the Holy Trinity is "known in one Godhead and one Monarchy, but in which Each of the three Divine Persons indwells and is indwelt by the Others." The eternal *perichoresis* of the three Persons, the "coinhering and coindwelling" of the Father, Son, and Holy Spirit, is the foundation on which to understand the mission of the Holy Spirit from the Father and the gift of the Holy Spirit by the Son. Thus, the Creed's third article is emphasized, for "it is precisely with the doctrine of the consubstantiality and Deity of the Holy Spirit that the proper understanding of the Holy Trinity is brought to its completion in the theology and worship of the Church." Once again, Western worry that the Holy Spirit can be seen as a free-floating presence, detached from Christ, is relieved by the affirmation of a fully orbed understanding of the Trinity — the One God, Father, Son, and Holy Spirit.

One Being, Three Persons

The Agreed Statement now circles back to its first section, reiterating that the doctrine of the Trinity does not proceed from any preconception or abstract definition of God's Being. To the contrary, it resets on "the very Being of God as he has named himself *'I am who I am/I shall be who I shall be'* (Exodus 3:14), the ever-living and self-revealing God." Similarly, the faith and confession of Unity in Trinity and Trinity in Unity does not rest on abstract definitions of divine relations, but on "the one revelation of God the Father which is given us through Jesus Christ and his Spirit."

The Apostolic and Catholic Faith

The Agreed Statement concludes with a resounding affirmation of Athanasius' declaration that "it is the very tradition, teaching and faith of the Catholic Church from the beginning, which the Lord gave, the Apostles preached, and the Fathers kept upon which the Church is founded . . . that there is a Trinity, Holy and complete . . . Thus the unity of the Holy Trinity is preserved and the One God is preached in the Church . . . It is a Trinity not only in name and form of speech, but in truth and reality."

"Significant Features: A Common Reflection on the Agreed Statement"

On the face of it, the Agreed Statement on the Holy Trinity is an extraordinary theological and ecumenical achievement. But what did the dialogue members themselves think they had done? Their "Common Reflection" provides some indication, for it identifies four significant features of the Agreed Statement. These four elements were stressed so that the churches would not miss them in the denser formulations of the Agreed Statement itself.

First, and most basic, the entire theological orientation of the Agreed Statement is governed by the fact that it is "only through God that God may be known."[38] The doctrine of the Trinity is not the product of human speculation or abstract calculation. The doctrine of the Trinity is not open to modern revision. Rather, "the self-revelation of God as the Father, the Son, and the Holy Spirit provides the framework within which alone it is to be interpreted."

Trinitarian Language

Attention is drawn to the Agreed Statement's recognition that "human language when applied to God is inevitably and rightly stretched beyond its ordinary or conventional sense." The doctrine of the Trinity, as well as all language about God, does not begin with standard definitions that then shape our understanding of God. Rather, borrowed terms such as οὐσια, ὑπόστασις, and φύσις (as well as *Father, Son,* and *Holy Spirit*) "are consistently handled in the new shape given to them as they are harnessed in the service of God's Trinitarian self-revelation." The Common Statement appears to draw on the Orthodox understanding of icons to signify the function of Trinitarian language: "Any images taken from creaturely being have to be understood in a diaphanous or 'see-through' way, in which they are used like lenses through which vision of truth may take place, but which are not themselves projected into Deity."

The Monarchy

The Common Statement emphasizes the monarchy of the Godhead in which all three divine Persons share. Because "there are not degrees of divinity in the Holy Trinity . . . any notion of subordination in God is completely ruled out." Contrary to both sophisticated and popular conceptions of modalism, the Common Statement underscores the principle that "the whole Being of God belongs to each divine Person as it belongs to all of them and belongs to all of them as it belongs to each of them." Agreement that the monarchy is not limited to one Person, in concert with the doctrine of the *perichoresis* of the three Persons, contributes to bridging the di-

---

38. Gros, Meyer, and Rusch, eds., *Growth in Agreement II*, 285. This and all subsequent quotations from the Common Reflection are taken from the text of "Significant Features: A Common Reflection on the Agreed Statement" on pages 285-287 of *Growth in Agreement II*.

vision between East and West over the *filioque,* "for it does not allow of any idea of the procession of the Spirit from two ultimate principles or αρχαί."

Ecumenical Significance

Because the Agreed Statement on the Holy Trinity moves neither from the three Persons to the one Being of God, nor from the one Being of God to the three Persons, it cuts across mistaken, polarized "Latin-Greek" approaches. The Common Statement concludes with the affirmation that "What is provided by the agreed statement of the Orthodox theologians in the East and the Reformed theologians in the West is preeminently a statement on the tri-unity of God as Trinity in unity and unity in Trinity."

From Agreed Statement on the Holy Trinity to Agreed Statement on Christology

Just as the Councils of Nicaea and Constantinople led to the Councils of Ephesus, Chalcedon, and beyond, so the "Agreed Statement on the Holy Trinity" led to the "Agreed Statement on Christology." The latter statement, agreed to at Limassol, Cyprus, a mere two years after the Trinity statement, was only possible because of fundamental Orthodox-Reformed accord on the Trinity. Yet even though the Agreed Statement on Christology affirmed "the basic interconnection between the doctrine of the Trinity and the doctrine of Christ,"[39] contrasts between Orthodox and Reformed theology begin to appear in the text.

As early as its second paragraph, the Agreed Statement on Christology notes that "Orthodox and Reformed seem to follow two different kinds of approach which, however, are not incompatible." Later in the text, differences between Orthodox *theosis* and Reformed *sanctification* are noted, but quickly glossed over. Even when agreement is articulated, the "we confess together" of the Agreed Statement on the Holy Trinity is replaced by "Orthodox and Reformed confess"; "is normative for both the Orthodox and Reformed traditions"; and "both Orthodox and Reformed recognize."

---

39. Gros, Meyer, and Rusch, eds., *Growth in Agreement II,* 288. This and all subsequent quotations from the Agreed Statement are taken from the text of the "Agreed Statement on Christology" on pages 188-290 of *Growth in Agreement II.*

The difference in tone is striking. Whereas the Trinity statement sought always to resolve distinctive emphases within a shared articulation, the Christology statement was content to set Reformed and Orthodox views side by side.

One wishes that the dialogue had taken the text as one step in a longer process, working to produce an Agreed Statement on Christology that bore the marks of a genuinely common testimony. Just as the meticulous preparation, thorough review and revision, and precise articulation of the Trinity statement made the Christology statement possible, similar preparation, review, and articulation would have made the Christology statement a more adequate basis for further dialogues.

Subsequent Orthodox-Reformed dialogues have not fulfilled the promise of the Agreed Statement on the Holy Trinity. Common (not agreed) statements on "The Church as the Body of Christ" (1998), "Membership and Incorporation into the Body of Christ" (2000), "The Holiness of the Church" (2003), and "The Catholicity and Mission of the Church" (2005) bear the marks of "comparative ecclesiology," setting forth Orthodox and Reformed views in alternating paragraphs, complete with mutual critique as well as common understanding. While this approach has the value of deepening mutual awareness and enrichment, it avoids the more demanding work of struggling to approach, or even achieve the possibility of saying, "We confess together the evangelical and ancient faith of the catholic church . . ."

A dramatic difference between the Agreed Statement on the Holy Trinity and all subsequent statements is the absence of patristic references from considerations of Christology and ecclesiology. For whatever reason, the careful attention to the Fathers that was so characteristic of the Trinity statement is utterly lacking. The silencing of voices from the formative centuries of the apostolic faith results in curiously abstract formulations that fail to address perennial theological issues.

Repeated Orthodox proposals for all churches to join in protracted exploration of patristic sources have been met with faint enthusiasm. The Orthodox-Reformed Agreed Statement on the Holy Spirit is dramatic evidence that such exploration can be fruitful as well as faithful. Attention to the church's early centuries is not antiquarian interest in the history of the doctrine. Ecumenical Patriarch Bartholomew has expressed a far more dynamic view of engagement with the Fathers. For Bartholomew, theology is not something acquired through research and study. Neither is it the result of authoritative declarations or arbitrary personal opinions. "Rather," he says, "it is the fruit of a communal conscience and consensus."[40] At its best, ecumenical dialogue aims beyond mutual understanding and common statements toward the fruit of communal conscience and consensus. How, then, does communal conscience and consensus develop? Bartholomew goes on to explain that "The very idea of theology, at least in the mind of the Orthodox Church, emerges out of the study of the Church Fathers. The foundation of Orthodox theology rests firmly on the tradition of the Church Fathers, namely on those whose inspiration and instruction have formed the conscience of the Church through the ages."[41]

Unfortunately, Reformed attention to the Fathers has become restricted to the back rooms of the academy, having little impact on theological work or church life. One ironic result of neglecting the Fathers is that it fosters an engagement with Scripture that leaps back over nineteen centuries to study texts that are detached from the ongoing life of the church. The Ecumenical Patriarchate serves the whole church when it persists in calling for engagement with those theologians of the early church whose fidelity to the faith of the apostles gave shape to the whole church's faith and faithfulness.

Wisdom's House

The icon collection of the Tretyakov Gallery in Moscow includes a profound mid-sixteenth-century icon, "Wisdom Hath Builded Her House." The icon alludes to Proverbs 9:1-6:

> Wisdom has built her house, she has set up her seven pillars.
> She has slaughtered her beasts, she has mixed her wine,
>   she has also set her table.
> She has sent out her maids to call from the highest places
>   in the town,
>   "Whoever is simple, let him turn in here!"
> To him who is without sense she says,
>   "Come, eat of my bread and drink of the wine I have mixed.
>   Leave simpleness, and live, and walk in the way of insight."

The upper part of the icon shows a row of six domed churches with one larger church behind and above them, together representing the seven Ec-

---

40. Bartholomew, *Encountering the Mystery*, 37.
41. Bartholomew, *Encountering the Mystery*, 38.

umenical Councils. Above the churches are seven angels, representing the gift of the Holy Spirit to the councils. Below and to the left Wisdom is enthroned in the circle of heaven, surrounded by symbols of the four evangelists. To the right of Wisdom, Solomon unfolds a scroll containing the text of Proverbs 6:1, and points to Mary and the Child Jesus, the new center of wisdom. The lower portion of the icon shows the preparation of a sacrifice, the setting of a table with bread and wine, and the serving of the Eucharist to people whose arms are eagerly outstretched.

This insightful icon sets forth the shape of the whole Church's Trinitarian faith. Scripture, both Old and New Testaments, is the foundation of the seven-pillared house of faith. This house — the seven Ecumenical Councils living out the trajectory of Nicaea — provides the Church with the vocabulary, grammar, and syntax of faith in the One God, Father, Son, and Holy Spirit. This Trinitarian faith, lived out in the Eucharist, forms, nourishes, and sustains the Church. The icon beckons all to "live and walk in the way of insight."

The Orthodox-Reformed "Agreed Statement on the Holy Trinity" can itself serve as an icon that calls out to the churches, "Turn in here, eat bread and wine, and walk together in the way of insight."

CHAPTER 7

Ecumenical Patriarch Bartholomew: A Committed Ecumenist

Mary Tanner

Looking back over the last fifty years of the work of the Faith and Order Commission of the World Council of Churches, it is striking to see the involvement of many of those who are today leaders in their own communions and who carry a major responsibility for the ministry of unity. Joseph Ratzinger, now Pope Benedict XVI, was one of the first Roman Catholic members of the Faith and Order Commission, though not a full member of the WCC itself. After the meeting of the Plenary Commission of Faith and Order in Louvain, Belgium, in 1971, Ratzinger wrote movingly about his experience and how he was impressed by a shared hope that permeated the meeting, its shared life of prayer, and the generous trust he found among the participants. He remarked that something positive emerged for the Church and the world out of a seemingly chaotic meeting with so many different languages, religious traditions, and academic backgrounds.[1] Walter Kasper, to become Cardinal Walter Kasper, the president of the Pontifical Council for Christian Unity, was also one of the early Roman Catholic members of the Faith and Order Commission, contributing to its work on the Apostolic Faith Study. The Archbishop of Canterbury, Dr. Rowan Williams, was involved in the same study and later represented the Church in Wales at the Fifth World Conference on Faith and Order in Santiago de Compostela, Spain, in 1993. But of all the leaders of the churches today, no one has had such a long and sustained association with the work of Faith

---

1. *Joseph Ratzinger in* Communio, vol. 1: *The Unity of the Church*, ed. David L. Schindler (Grand Rapids: Eerdmans, 2010), 7.

and Order than the Ecumenical Patriarch His All Holiness Bartholomew. His involvement has extended over three periods of Faith and Order's work.

Metropolitan Bartholomew, Metropolitan of Philadelphia from the Ecumenical Patriarchate of Constantinople, became a member of the Commission in 1977. He was to continue as a member of the Plenary and Standing Commissions until he became Ecumenical Patriarch in 1991, attending his last meeting of the Standing Commission in Rome in the same year. From 1983 to 1990 Metropolitan Bartholomew served as a vice moderator of the Commission under the wise leadership of the American Methodist theologian Professor John Deschner. His fellow vice moderators, the Reverend Dr. Horace Russell (Baptist), Fr. Jean Tillard, O.P. (Roman Catholic), and I (Anglican), together with the director of Faith and Order, the Reverend Dr. Günther Gassmann (Lutheran), made up the officers' team helping to guide the work of the 121 members of the Plenary Commission and the 30 members of the Standing Commission. I am proud to have worked closely with His All Holiness Bartholomew for more than fourteen years, first as members of the Commission and then as vice moderators together. When I succeeded Professor John Deschner as moderator of the Commission I felt supported in my responsibilities by His All Holiness, although for obvious reasons he could no longer continue as a member of the Commission. I remember meeting the Ecumenical Patriarch when he paid an official visit to the Church of England and the first words with which he greeted me were "Ah, Faith and Order!" Was he reminding me of our shared work, or was it a wistful regret that he was no longer an active member of the Commission?

The years during which Metropolitan Bartholomew served on the Faith and Order Commission were extraordinarily fruitful years and were to prove of immense importance to the churches, producing a major contribution toward the visible unity of the church. One of the fundamental characteristics of the work of Faith and Order has been continuity, the faithful nurturing of the agenda set out in the First World Conference on Faith and Order in Lausanne in 1927 and summed up in Faith and Order's Constitution:

> To proclaim the oneness of the church of Jesus Christ and to call the churches to the goal of visible unity in one faith and Eucharistic fellowship, expressed in worship and in common life in Christ, in order that the world may believe.[2]

---

2. Cf. *Faith and Order at the Crossroads: Kuala Lumpur 2004*, Faith and Order Paper 196, ed. Thomas F. Best (Geneva: WCC Publications, 2005), 450ff.

Joining the Commission in 1977 meant that Metropolitan Bartholo-mew became involved in the work that flowed directly from the Plenary Commission meeting in Accra, Ghana, in 1973. Faith and Order had come to see that there were three requirements necessary for the visible unity of the Church: the common confession of the apostolic faith; one baptism, Eucharist, and a mutually recognized ministry; and ways of deciding and teaching with authority. The Accra meeting was to make progress in all three areas. It was the work of the first week of that meeting on "giving ac-count of the hope that is in us" that was to lead, some years later, to the study on the Common Confession of the Apostolic Faith, a study in which Metropolitan Bartholomew was himself to play a leading role as a member of its Steering Committee. But the most significant work of Accra was the finalizing of the Accra Text, *One Baptism, One Eucharist, and a Mutually Recognized Ministry.*[3] The Plenary Commission agreed in Accra that the texts did not yet represent a formal consensus. Nevertheless, they were of-fered to the churches as "significant instruments for achieving agreement in inter-confessional discussions at all levels." It was this work which was to develop into what is perhaps the most important ecumenical document of the ecumenical century, *Baptism, Eucharist, and Ministry (BEM),* the so-called Lima Text. The Accra meeting was important for convincing Faith and Order to continue emphasizing the inextricable relation between the unity of the Church and the unity of humankind and the need to study the unity of the Church in the context of human divisions so that church unity might be seen to have something to say to human divisions. The fact that the Commission was meeting for the first time in Africa and that there were more representatives from the developing countries, more women, and more lay theologians, meant that the insights of the Commission would be radically enriched in the years ahead. It was in Accra that the im-petus for the study on the Community of Women and Men in the Church came from a group trying to express its hope as a community of women and men in the Church. It was an exciting time for Faith and Order as the Commission faced the challenges not only of ecclesial tradition speaking to ecclesial tradition but of cultural context speaking to cultural context as well as the challenges from liberation movements.

---

3. *One Baptism, One Eucharist, and a Mutually Recognized Ministry,* Faith and Order Paper 73 (Geneva: WCC, 1974).

Phase 1: 1977-1982

This was the context in which a young Metropolitan Bartholomew became a member of the Standing and Plenary Commissions. The Commission had just celebrated the fiftieth anniversary of the First World Conference on Faith and Order in Lausanne, 1927, and had been given fresh direction in the memorable Accra meeting. The years ahead were to see important advances and were no doubt formative in Metropolitan Bartholomew's own ecumenical understanding and in strengthening his commitment. The new Commission's task at Loccum, Germany, in 1977, under its (Orthodox) moderator, Professor Nikos Nissiotis, an Orthodox theologian from Greece and director of the Ecumenical Institute of Bossey, was to review work accomplished since Accra and to lay firm plans for the plenary meeting the following year in Bangalore, India. The meeting, as always in Faith and Order, was sustained by a life of prayer. Each day's proceedings were opened with a period of prayer and at noon a service of intercessions focused on the concerns of churches in different parts of the world. A service of Holy Communion was celebrated at which all were invited to participate according to the disciplines of their own church. Such celebrations were both occasions of joy and times of pain and confusion as each struggled with the discipline of their own churches. This particular celebration was my first experience of being at a Eucharist presided over by a woman, a Lutheran pastor.

In drawing up plans for Bangalore, the Standing Commission wanted the Commission to have the same exposure to the Asian context as it had had of the African context in Accra. The focus of the meeting was to be the second stage of the account of hope study and the continuation of work on the goal of, and the way to, visible unity, including work on baptism, Eucharist, ministry, conciliar fellowship, and the contextual studies, particularly the study on the Community of Women and Men in the Church.

Metropolitan Bartholomew was at the meeting in Bangalore. Its most memorable achievement was the adoption of the statement, "A Common Account of Hope." It had been an ambitious project to try to express a common account of hope out of the diversity of confessions that the Commission listened to from around the world, not least of all from places of turmoil and apparent lack of hope: from Eastern Europe behind the Iron Curtain, to the apartheid of South Africa, to the hopelessness of sectarian violence in Northern Ireland. It was, as the director of Faith and Order, the Reverend Dr. Lukas Vischer, admitted after the meeting, "a hazardous undertaking." The difference had to be overcome between those who looked for an account of the gospel message in the victory of Jesus who has overcome the world, and those who wanted the emphasis to be on concrete situations where hope is bravely expressed now, "hope against hope." Slowly and laboriously, a common account of hope did take shape so that on the final morning when yet another revised version was read out the Commission members rose to their feet and broke spontaneously into prolonged applause for a statement in which each could recognize themselves. No one who was at that meeting could possibly forget that moment, which demonstrated that "Christians from the most diverse traditions were able to give an agreed account of the wellsprings of their life as Christians."[4]

The second major theme of the meeting was the unity of the church. The Commission was convinced that it needed in the future to focus upon the three requirements for visible unity: the apostolic faith; the work towards consensus on baptism, Eucharist, and ministry (deepening the convergences in conversation with the churches around the Accra Text); and structures for common teaching and decision-making. Although Bangalore did not focus on the theme of the Unity of the Church, the Unity of Mankind, it was clear from the work on the account of hope, as well as in the developing study on the Community of Women and Men in the Church, that this overall framework and vision was essential for all aspects of Faith and Order's work. But there was then, and remains, a tension between those who tend to believe that all emphasis should be on the production of consensus statements on the three requirements for visible unity and on the other hand those who want to lay the emphasis upon the form and quality of life in fellowship today. The interaction of those with different emphases and priorities was to prove one of the most difficult but potentially most creative tensions for the future work of the Commission. Whenever polarization was avoided and the insights of both were brought together, something fruitful emerged.

Following Bangalore, the Standing Committee met in Taizé, France, in 1979. Again its work was grounded in shared worship in the morning, at midday, and in the evening with the Community. The Commission was present at a Eucharist in the Community Church of the Reconciliation presided over by Frère Max Thurian, to become a leader in the process around the work on baptism, Eucharist, and ministry in the years to come,

---

4. *Sharing in One Hope,* Faith and Order Paper 92 (Geneva: WCC, 1978), viii.

and there were fascinating times of exchange with Frère Roger Schutz, the head of the Community.

But Taizé was not an easy meeting, as the letter to the officers and members of the Executive Committee of the World Council of Churches published in the minutes shows.[5] The Council had determined that no member of staff should serve for more than nine years. This meant that the leadership of Dr. Lukas Vischer, who had served Faith and Order for eighteen years with energy and insight, would come to an end. Faith and Order, whose membership was broader than the membership of the Council itself, was concerned that the initiative for appointing members of staff should remain in the hands of the Commission and that, if a name submitted by the Commission were to fail in the Executive Committee, then Faith and Order should be invited to offer a further name. The difficulties over the process of appointment were symptomatic of an ongoing tension between the Commission and the Council. Because of its broader membership, Faith and Order was rightly anxious to retain a certain degree of autonomy in matters of finance, staffing, and program, while being interdependent in the life of the Council. It is worth recalling this as it illustrates the tension that surfaces from time to time between the Commission and the Council. It was in delicate matters such as these that Metropolitan Bartholomew came to play a reconciling role, always offering wise counsel to the officers and to the Commission.

In Taizé plans were laid for the next plenary meeting to be held, for the first time, in Latin America. In preparation for that meeting, the conversation with the churches around the Accra Text on baptism, Eucharist, and ministry would continue and, in the light of responses from the churches as well as insights from specialist consultations on baptism, on *episcope* and episcopacy, and the ordination of women, a small drafting team was to prepare a more mature text. The minutes of the Taizé meeting show another growing and important emphasis in the work of Faith and Order: the theme of koinonia. Professor Wolfhart Pannenberg, commenting on the work on the Unity of the Church and the Unity of Humankind (no longer *mankind*), suggested that "only to the degree of the spiritual credibility of the churches could they contribute to the general problems of the unity of humankind . . . greater emphasis should be placed on communion/ *koinonia* . . . By using the term the documents could deal with the unity of

5. *Minutes of the Meeting of the Standing Commission, 1979, Taize* (Geneva: WCC, 1980), 89-90.

the Church and the unity of humankind at the same time. Christ is the new Adam; we share in that eschatological reality as we have *koinonia*."[6]

No one who was at the meeting in Lima in 1982 will ever forget the moment at which, after many last-minute revisions to the text, the vice moderator, John Deschner, put to the Commission that Faith and Order's revised text, *Baptism, Eucharist, and Ministry (BEM)*, was "mature enough to be sent to all the churches for reception and official response." He called for a vote. The motion was passed unanimously, no negative votes and no abstentions. Metropolitan Bartholomew was among those who affirmed the Lima Text.[7] The Commission rose to its feet in silent prayer. As Michael Kinnamon, one of the members of the staff of Faith and Order, wrote at the time, "History may show this to be one of the most significant moments of the modern ecumenical movement."[8] That unanimous vote marked the end of a study process that had begun in 1927 at the First World Conference. It also marked the first time theologians from such varied backgrounds had spoken harmoniously on fundamental matters of doctrine. For the past five years of intensive work Metropolitan Bartholomew had been close to this process and contributed, together with Professor Nikos Nissiotis and other Orthodox members of the Commission, a deep Orthodox perspective which infused the convergence text of *BEM*.

When the decision was made the Commission was staying in a retreat center at the Oasis de los Santos Apostoles, just outside Lima. The lush vegetation of the oasis stood in stark contrast to the barren hills that rose on every side. Where the green gave way to barrenness, there were a few half-built shacks where the poor of Lima, unimaginably poor, eked out some existence. Here were the churches in their comfortable oasis, safeguarding their life-giving traditions of baptism, Eucharist, and ministry; and there outside a world of starvation and death. The wonderful thing was that the tension in the Commission between those who looked for unearthed doctrinal documents and those for whom cultural context was prior had proved a creative tension. The struggles in the Commission experienced in Africa, Asia, and now Latin America had borne fruit in the vision of the Lima Text, seen in its inclusive language for the community of faith, and in its linking of the healing power of sacramental grace in situa-

6. *Minutes of the Meeting of the Standing Commission*, 17, 19.

7. *Baptism, Eucharist, and Ministry*, Faith and Order Paper 111 (Geneva: WCC, 1982).

8. Michael Kinnamon, "Preface, 1," in *Towards Visible Unity: Commission on Faith and Order, Lima 1982*, vol. 1: *Minutes and Addresses*, Faith and Order Paper 123 (Geneva: WCC, 1982).

tions of injustice and brokenness, nowhere more clearly expressed than in Paragraph 20 of the Eucharist text:

> The eucharistic celebration demands reconciliation and sharing among all those regarded as brothers and sisters in the one family of God and is a constant challenge in the search for appropriate relationships in social, economic and political life . . . All kinds of injustice, racism, separation and lack of freedom are radically challenged when we share in the body and blood of Christ.

The Lima meeting was not only important for setting in motion an intensive interactive process of engagement with churches around the Lima Text, which was to be ably overseen by Frère Max Thurian of the Taizé Community, but also for the plans laid for the new study, "Towards a Common Confession of the Apostolic Faith Today."

The First World Conference on Faith and Order in 1927 had posed the question, "What degree of unity in faith will be necessary in a reunited Church?" Already contemporary accounts of faith had been collected by the Commission from around the world. The question faced now at Lima was one of methodological approach, including what role the Nicene-Constantinopolitan Creed (381) (NCC), should play in the study. There were those who held the NCC to be the universally orthodox expression of the apostolic faith and those who held it to be a product of a moment in history, now outmoded and having no obvious relationship to ethical conduct today. An Anglican from Latin America, the Reverend Dr. Jaci Maraschin, expressed it most powerfully: "Christians in Latin America confess their faith as a system of formal dogmatic propositions, accepted reason, or as a cry for the struggle in favor of the oppressed and poor." He identified the former with "the colonizers and the powerful." The Christian faith, he contended, is not a system, though it has often been systematized. It is, rather, a living experience, confessed by a living community at a specific time and in a specific culture. Therefore, he went on, "we from this part of the world ask Faith and Order if it is possible to confess our faith through a common expression taking as a base an ancient document built upon a very specific frame of reference and addressed in a very particular language code which in its essence is alien to us in our place and time."[9] This was a sharp challenge.

---

9. *Towards Visible Unity*, 92.

In addition to the continuing work around *BEM* and the Apostolic Faith Study, plans were made for a new major study on the Unity of the Church and the Renewal of Human Community, building on insights from the past. This first phase of Metropolitan Bartholomew's involvement with Faith and Order between 1977 and 1982 was during a creative time for the Commission, The more representative nature of the Commission, the impact of meetings in Africa, Asia, and Latin America, and the influence of liberation theologies raised new challenges and new possibilities for the work of Faith and Order. At best the tensions between the classical and contextual methods proved fruitful, as the Lima Text illustrates. The vision of visible unity was aware of the advances being made in the churches: the work of the bilateral conversations, new forms of closer ecumenical cooperation at the local level, more action together through councils of churches in many parts of the world, and the progress of the United and Uniting churches.

Phase 2: 1983-1990

In Taizé, in 1979, Metropolitan Bartholomew had extended an invitation to the Standing Commission to meet in the beautiful Orthodox Academy in Crete; this is where the newly appointed Standing Commission gathered in 1984. The Orthodox Academy was to host a number of Faith and Order consultations in the years to come. The director of the Academy, Dr. Alexandros Papaderos, was a generous host and was to prove so on a number of future occasions.[10]

The meeting in Crete marked the beginning of a new phase in the work of the Commission in what its new director, Günther Gassmann, described as a "joyful, cooperative, and creative spirit." This was the meeting at which Metropolitan Bartholomew was elected as one of the vice moderators of the Commission and a member of the steering group for the Apostolic Faith Study. It was in this small steering group in Crete that the main outline of the study was hammered out. Not an easy task, it was clear that there was no intention to write a new Creed. Rather, the plan was to take the NCC, the ancient and most widely used confession of faith today, and to examine how the faith of the Creed is grounded in the biblical witness

---

10. *Minutes of the Meeting of the Standing Commission 1984, Crete,* Faith and Order Paper 121 (Geneva: WCC, 1984), 67.

and how that faith is both challenged, and challenges us, today. This was to lead to an explication of the faith of the Creed, which might help the divided churches recognize in their own lives and in the lives of others a shared fidelity to the same apostolic faith. All of this was to help divided churches come together to make common confession of the one faith, as a sign of their unity in faith.

At the Commission meeting in Lima, John Deschner had urged that it was time to consider calling a Fifth World Conference on Faith and Order. Already twenty years had passed since the Fourth World Conference in Montreal. He spoke of throwing out an anchor and drawing ourselves and our work as the Commission toward the anchor. At Crete the proposal became firm and the date set for 1988 or 1989. A World Conference could have a greater impact on the churches than any meeting of the Commission itself and provide an opportunity to set before the churches the recent work on apostolic faith, baptism, Eucharist, and ministry and common ways of decision making and teaching with authority and on the unity of the Church and the renewal of human community. The Conference would be a moment of truth and hopefully provide an opportunity for a renewed commitment to the unity of the Church.

The work of this phase of the Commission's life, through two Plenary Commission meetings, one in Stavanger, Norway, and the other in Budapest, focused on three main studies: the maturing of the Apostolic Faith Study, the overseeing of the BEM process, and the Unity of the Church and the Renewal of Human Community. All the time in the background was the thought that these studies were in some way being prepared for presentation at a Fifth World Conference. Metropolitan Bartholomew continued to take a major interest in the Apostolic Faith Study, attending many of the steering committee meetings and taking part in one of the specialist consultations on the second article of the Creed: Confessing the Crucified and Risen Christ in the Social, Cultural, and Ethical Context of Today. The consultation was held in Rhodes, where the participants joined in the memorable Orthodox celebration of the Feast of the Epiphany. These years concentrated on producing an explication of the faith of the Creed. "The goal of explication," as the director of Faith and Order explained to the Commission in Stavanger,

> was to achieve a common reappropriation of the basic convictions of our faith for the present time. This could then pave the way both for the recognition of the ancient creeds of the Church as fundamental state-

ments of the apostolic faith, and for a common witness to the faith whenever Christians and churches are summoned to such witness in specific situations in our world today.[11]

Many fine papers were read by leading theologians at the consultations on the three articles of the Creed. The text that resulted, *Confessing the One Faith: An Ecumenical Explication of the Apostolic Faith as It Is Confessed in the Nicene-Constantinopolitan Creed (381) (COF),* was on any reckoning an impressive achievement.[12] It was prepared by the staff person responsible for the project, the Reverend Dr. Gennadios Limouris, himself a constant support to Metropolitan Bartholomew. The explication was to serve as an instrument for a move to mutual recognition. Its publication was complemented by six volumes of contemporary confessions of faith from around the world.

Perhaps because the churches were still deeply into the process of responding to the Lima Text, *Baptism, Eucharist, and Ministry, COF* never received the enthusiastic response of that earlier study that it deserved. But it has become a major resource in many seminaries and universities in the teaching of doctrine and was republished in 2010.

The second emphasis of these years was monitoring the continuing process around the Lima Text. By the time of the Budapest Plenary Meeting, seven had passed since the completion of *Baptism, Eucharist, and Ministry.* The Commission had prepared a comprehensive summary and evaluation of the process and the responses to date. *BEM* had become the most widely distributed, translated, and discussed ecumenical text in modern times. Some 450,000 copies had been published, translations made into 31 languages, and over 1,000 responses received, among them 180 official responses from churches. "Never before have so many from theological faculties, confessional families, ecumenical groups, local congregations, and discussion groups of lay and ordained persons joined together in studying the same modern ecumenical document." Faith and Order published six volumes of church responses and then prepared a response to the responses.[13]

---

11. *Faith and Renewal, Commission of Faith and Order, Stavanger 1985,* Faith and Order paper 131 (Geneva: WCC, 1985), 34.

12. *Confessing the One Faith: An Ecumenical Explication of the Apostolic Faith as It Is Confessed in the Nicene-Constantinopolitan Creed (381),* Faith and Order Paper 153 (Geneva: WCC, 1991).

13. See for example, Max Thurian, ed., *Churches Respond to BEM: Official Responses to*

Work on the Unity of the Church and Renewal of Human Community continued to provide an important context for all of Faith and Order's work and more than should have been of strategic importance for all the work of the World Council of Churches. Often the unity of the church and the renewal of human community are seen as separate and competing agendas, yet "this study was to demonstrate theologically the way in which these two emphases are organically interrelated." This was easier to state as an aim but harder to follow through. One central aspect of the study, important for later work on ecclesiology, was the reflection on the church as mystery and prophetic sign.

Although Metropolitan Bartholomew was primarily concerned with the Apostolic Faith Study, it was impossible to be part of the team of vice moderators without sharing some overall responsibility for all three programs. It was in the meetings of the officers' team, often going late into the night, that once more Metropolitan Bartholomew was to show his pastoral concern for overworked staff and was a reconciler in times of tension and frustrations. He was never afraid to confront hard situations, but always did so with the heart of a pastor, with gentleness and wisdom.

It was in Lima that the impetus had come for a Fifth World Conference, to present the churches with the work of Faith and Order, to hear their reactions, and to lay directions together for the future. The general secretary of the WCC, the Reverend Dr. Emilio Castro, at the meeting of the Plenary Commission in Stavanger in 1985 was both critical of Faith and Order's plans for a World Conference and challenging. "I am quite excited about it . . . but I am also afraid."[14] He believed that the message so far expressed from Faith and Order for a World Conference was unlikely to capture the imaginations or enthusiasm of the churches. He wanted a much more significant event than Faith and Order had dared to envisage so far. By the next time the Plenary Commission met in Budapest in 1989 plans were beginning to be clearer for a World Conference. The date set was 1993, exactly thirty years after the Fourth World Conference, with the theme "Towards a Credible Communion in Faith, Life, and Witness." This theme would allow for a comprehensive theological discourse on the present and future of the ecumenical vision, while enabling participants to re-

---

"*Baptism, Eucharist and Ministry" Text*, vol. 1, Faith and Order Paper 129 (Geneva: WCC Publications, 1986), and *Baptism, Eucharist, and Ministry: Report on the Process and Responses*, Faith and Order Paper 149 (Geneva: WCC Publications, 1990).

14. Thurian, *Churches Respond to BEM*, 60.

flect on present Faith and Order studies. Looking back, it is easy to see that since Lima the Commission had increasingly been concerned not only with separate studies but with a more holistic approach to ecclesiology. As Günther Gassmann told the Commission, "The overarching theme of ecclesiology would not only serve as a basis for dealing with controversial issues and the understanding of the church as a whole, but also as the theological context in which the pressing issues of church-world relationship can be considered in a more theologically focused way than has often been the case."[15]

The direction of the Commission's work on ecclesiology was greatly influenced by a seminal paper Metropolitan John Zizioulas of Pergamon delivered at Budapest, which he began by saying that ecclesiology is a subject which is paradoxically both omnipresent in ecumenical discussion and at the same time absent from it:

> Because there can hardly be any discussion of problems pertaining to church unity without an implicit or explicit reference to the nature of the church . . . no attempt has been made so far to see to what extent there is convergence or divergence among the churches . . . concerning their views on what the church is . . . The study of ecclesiology cannot be postponed for too long.

Metropolitan John went on to remind the Commission that many of the official responses to *BEM* identified the need for a study of ecclesiology. Metropolitan John insisted that the identity of the church is relational and that we cannot understand the church apart from relationship with God and relation to the particular place in which the church is brought into relationship with actual realities of the world. This double perspective — a biblical perspective — ought to be the basic one in any ecclesiology. He went on to explore the church as a reflection of God's way of being. At this point Trinitarian theology becomes a *sine qua non*. The direction Metropolitan John was indicating for the study of ecclesiology brought together many of the contributions of Orthodox members of the Commission over many years, not least of all those from Professor Nikos Nissiotis, Metropolitan Bartholomew, and Professor Nicholas Lossky. The theme of koinonia in particular was to become the inspiration for the work on ecclesiology. It was to be a major influence in both the eventual theme chosen for the

---

15. *Faith and Order 1985-1989: The Commission Meeting at Budapest,* Faith and Order Paper 148 (Geneva: WCC, 1990), 7.

World Conference — "Towards Koinina in Faith, Life, and Witness" — as well as in the unity statement drafted by the Commission for the Vancouver Assembly in 1991, *The Unity of the Church as* Koinonia: *Gift and Calling*. It was also found in the first draft of the ecclesiology text, *Nature and Mission of the Church.*[16]

Phase 3: 1991-2011

Metropolitan Bartholomew, now Senior Metropolitan of Chalcedon, was appointed for a third term as an Orthodox member of Faith and Order, attending the first meeting of the newly appointed Standing Commission in Rome in 1991. This was my first meeting as moderator; it was also the last meeting that Metropolitan Bartholomew would attend as a member. A few months later, on 22 October, he was elected Ecumenical Patriarch.

Not surprisingly, much of that Commission's time now had to be spent on preparations for the World Conference, only two years away. But another matter was on the mind of Faith and Order, one concerning Metropolitan Bartholomew at the time of the Rome meeting. At the Assembly of the World Council in Canberra the reflections on the theme of the Assembly, "Come Holy Spirit, Renew the Whole Creation," by Professor Chung Hyun Kyung, a young woman theologian from Korea, made many deeply unhappy, and not only the Orthodox participants. It brought into the open a concern that often the Orthodox voice and perspectives on issues seemed to be ignored. The Orthodox were not the only ones to feel this. Anglicans had on a number of occasions felt that their concerns were not always heard. In Canberra this was particularly felt not over an ecclesiological issue, but over the Statement on the Gulf War.

Fr. Jean Tillard, one of the vice moderators of Faith and Order, always a perceptive observer of matters in the Council, explained to the Standing Commission in Rome that something new had happened in Canberra, something of extreme importance for Faith and Order.[17] An alliance had been forged between the Roman Catholics, the Orthodox, and the evangelicals, "something new and crucial for Faith and Order." These three groups were calling for a reform of the World Council of Churches around the spe-

16. *Nature and Mission of the Church*, Faith and Order Paper 198 (Geneva: WCC, 2005).
17. *Minutes of the Meeting of the Faith and Order Standing Commission, Rome, Italy, 1991*, Faith and Order Paper 157 (Geneva: WCC, 1991), 17ff.

cific goals of Faith and Order. He described how some of his Orthodox friends — he names none of them and so it is unclear whether Metropolitan Bartholomew, who was certainly at Canberra, was among them — in a very dramatic evening, expressed a wish to leave the Council. Metropolitan Bartholomew, as head of the delegation of the Ecumenical Patriarchate, subsequently called for an extraordinary meeting of all the heads of the Eastern and Oriental Orthodox delegation. After a lengthy consultation and serious reflection, it was unanimously decided that if there was not any official reaction from the Council, then the Orthodox should leave the Assembly. The future of the Council, they felt, depended "on the way the WCC will take seriously the goals of Faith and Order . . . You must not be absorbed but keep the amount of autonomy you need to be what you are supposed to be, and not what the WCC wants you to be." The drama of Canberra was that Faith and Order seemed to have no specific room in the whole meeting. Fr. Jean believed that the new program on ecclesiology would need to answer the burning questions that surfaced at Canberra, namely, "the tension between unity and catholicity." It was largely the reaction of the Orthodox at Canberra that led to the setting up of the Special Commission on Orthodox Participation in the World Council of Churches, which was to produce important and reconciling new directions for the work of the fellowship of churches.

Perhaps it was at the Rome meeting of the Faith and Order Standing Commission that Metropolitan Bartholomew came to understand, as others did, the urgency of the questions being raised by the Orthodox and how these issues related closely to the role of Faith and Order and its work on ecclesiology. In the years that followed, although no longer a member of the Commission, His All Holiness continued to show support for the work of the World Council of Churches — not least of all the work of the Special Commission on Orthodox Participation, as well as the ongoing work of Faith and Order.

His All Holiness sent a message to the Fifth World Conference in Santiago de Compostela, with its ecclesiological theme "Towards *Koinonia* in Faith, Life, and Witness":

> Our Church of Constantinople, which has been involved in the ecumenical movement from the beginning and has served continuously the ecumenical goal and vision of Church unity, will not cease to be committed to the efforts of Faith and Order, through its prayers as well as the contribution of its delegation . . . it is our sincere hope that your

common consideration of "*Koinonia* in Faith, Life, and Witness" may add decisively to all our previous efforts to receive together the divine gift of Church unity so that diversity among us may cease to be divisive and become, as at Pentecost, a living witness to the same redemptive reality.[18]

In light of the constant support for Faith and Order and its place within the World Council of Churches it was especially appropriate that the final meeting of the Standing Commission of this period of Faith and Order's work took place at the gracious invitation of His All Holiness Bartholomew in Istanbul. The sessions were held in the recently restored Holy Monastery of Balouki, where His Eminence Metropolitan Professor Dr. Gennadios of Assima — a onetime member of the staff of Faith and Order, who had contributed much to the Apostolic Faith Study and to the early preparations for the meeting in Santiago de Compostela, Spain — exhibited a ministry of diakonia which left a lasting impression on all of us. The Commission was received in an audience with His All Holiness. As moderator of the Commission I presented Patriarch Bartholomew with a photo of the Rome meeting, expressing the hope that he would put it side by side with the photo just taken of this meeting, to recall his deep involvement with the Commission over so many years. His All Holiness urged Faith and Order "to call the churches to the goal of visible unity with ever greater persistence."[19] It was a happy and memorable meeting with the Ecumenical Patriarch at which the past was recalled and old friendships renewed.

It is right that these reflections on the involvement of His All Holiness with the work of Faith and Order should be brought to a close with reference to his presence at the most recent meeting of the Plenary Commission of Faith and Order at the Orthodox Academy of Crete, in Greece, in 2009 — the place where he had taken the Commission to meet all those years ago. In his opening address, entitled "Unity as Calling, Conversion, and Mission," he began by welcoming the participants of our "beloved Faith and Order Commission . . . to our Orthodox Academy on this uniquely beautiful island." He urged the Commission, "Let us renew our commitment to dialogue and unity as a way of reflection and renewal. And

18. *On the Way to Fuller Koinonia: Official Report of the Fifth World Conference on Faith and Order*, Faith and Order Paper 166 (Geneva: WCC, 1993), 209, 300.

19. *Minutes of the Meeting of the Faith and Order Board, 9-16 January 1998, Istanbul, Turkey*, Faith and Order Paper 180 (Geneva: WCC, 1998), 125ff.

let our deliberation be a prayerful offering to God in our sincere desire that 'we may be one.'"[20]

The address was grounded in Orthodox spirituality, the teaching of the Fathers and Mothers of the Church, and with a passion for unity in mission. His All Holiness summed up his address in these words:

> Beloved brothers and sisters, the unity that we seek is a gift from above, which we must pursue persistently as well as patiently: it is not something that depends solely on us, but primarily on God's judgment, *kairos*. Nevertheless, this sacred gift of unity is something that also demands of us radical conversion and reorientation so that we may turn humbly toward our common roots in the Apostolic Church and the communion of saints, but also so that we may entrust ourselves and submit to God's heavenly kingdom and authority. Finally, however, unity obliges us to a common purpose in this age-to-come; for it commits us to a sacred ministry and mission in realizing that kingdom, as we declare in the Lord's prayer, "on earth as in heaven." Such is the sacred gift that we have inherited. This, too, is the sacred task that lies before us.
>
> May the grace, peace, and love of God be with all of you.

It remained only for the Communion then, as I do now, to express deep gratitude for the enormous contribution, inspiration, and the continuing support that His All Holiness the Ecumenical Patriarch Bartholomew has shown to the work of Faith and Order over more than thirty years.

---

20. *Unity as Calling, Conversion, and Mission,* available online at www.wcc.org, and shortly to be published in the Minutes of the Crete Meeting of the Plenary Commission.

Contributors

ANNA MARIE AAGAARD, Professor Emerita of Systematic Theology in the University of Aarhus, Denmark, and a former President of the World Council of Churches, has been a member of the International Lutheran-Orthodox Dialogue and is the author of a number of articles dealing with ecumenical topics, including coauthor of a volume dealing with the relations of the Orthodox Churches to the World Council of Churches.

PETER C. BOUTENEFF is Associate Professor of Systematic Theology at Saint Vladimir's Orthodox Theological Seminary. From 1995 to 2000 he served as a staff member of the Communion on Faith and Order of the World Council of Churches. Since then he has served as a member of the Special Commission on Orthodox Participation in the World Council. He has coauthored a volume dealing with the relations of the Orthodox Churches to the World Council of Churches.

GÜNTHER GASSMANN is a German Lutheran theologian and ecumenist. He has been Research Professor at the Institute for Ecumenical Research in Strasbourg, France, President of the Central Office of the Lutheran Churches in Germany, and Director of the Commission on Faith and Order of the World Council of Churches, where he met Metropolitan Bartholomew many times. In his retirement he teaches in several faculties as visiting professor.

DALE T. IRVIN, President and Professor of World Christianity at New York Theological Seminary, is the author of several books, articles, and chapters. A member of Riverside Church in New York City, he is ordained in the American Baptist Churches.

RONALD G. ROBERSON, CSP, Associate Director of the Secretariat for Ecumenical and Interreligious Affairs, United States Conference of Catholic Bishops, Washington, D.C., is a member of the Oriental Orthodox–Roman Catholic International Dialogue and a member of the United States Orthodox-Catholic Dialogue. He served on the staff of the Pontifical Council for Promoting Christian Unity, Vatican City, from 1988 to 1992.

WILLIAM G. RUSCH, Adjunct Professor at Yale Divinity School and New York Theological Seminary, was Executive Director of the Office for Ecumenical Affairs of the Evangelical Lutheran Church in America and a member of the Commission on Faith and Order of the World Council of Churches and the National Council of Churches of Christ in the United States. He has authored several books and numerous articles on patristic and ecumenical themes.

JOSEPH D. SMALL served as Director of the Presbyterian Church (U.S.A.) Office of Theology and Worship from 1989 to 2011. He is now adjunct faculty at the University of Dubuque Theological Seminary, and church-relations consultant to the Presbyterian Foundation. He serves on the board of the Center for Catholic and Evangelical Theology, the Faith and Order Commission of the National Council of Churches of Christ in the United States, and is co-chair of the International Reformed-Pentecostal Dialogue. He has authored several works on ecumenical and interreligious topics.

MARY TANNER, currently the President (for Europe) of the World Council of Churches, served as a member of the Faith and Order Commission of the World Council of Churches from 1975 and as its Moderator from 1991 to 1998. As first General Secretary of the Church of England's Council for Christian Unity, she participated in the Anglican–Roman Catholic International Commission and other bilateral dialogues. Queen Elizabeth named her a Dame of the British Empire in 2007.